Secret
power

Secret power

D.L. MOODY

WHITAKER
HOUSE

All Scripture quotations are from the King James Version (KJV) of the Bible.

Editor's note: This book has been edited for the modern reader. Words, expressions, and sentence structure have been updated for clarity and readability.

SECRET POWER

ISBN: 0-88368-848-4
Printed in the United States of America
© 1997 by Whitaker House

Whitaker House
30 Hunt Valley Circle
New Kensington, PA 15068
web site: www.whitakerhouse.com

Library of Congress Cataloging-in-Publication Data

Moody, Dwight Lyman, 1837–1899.
  Secret power / D. L. Moody.
      p.   cm.
Originally published: New York: F. H. Revell, 1881.
  ISBN 0-88368-848-4
  1. Holy Spirit.   2. Baptism in the Holy Spirit.   3. Christian life.
I. Title.
  BT122 .M58 2002
  234'.13—dc21

                                    2002013608

1 2 3 4 5 6 7 8 9 10 11 12 / 09 08 07 06 05 04 03 02

Contents

Chapter One

Power—Its Source

Chapter One

Power—Its Source

*Without the soul, divinely quickened
and inspired, the observances of the grandest
ritualism are as worthless as the motions
of a galvanized corpse.*
—Anonymous

I begin with this quote because it leads me at once to the subject under consideration. What is this quickening and inspiration? What power is needed? What is its source? I reply, "The Holy Spirit of God." I am a full believer in the Apostles' Creed, and therefore, "I believe in the Holy Spirit."

A writer has pointedly asked, "What are our souls without His grace? As dead as the branch in which the sap does not circulate. What is the church without Him? As parched and barren as the fields without the dew and rain of heaven."

There has been much inquiry of late on the subject of the Holy Spirit. In this and other countries, thousands of people have been giving attention to the study of this grand theme. I hope it will lead us all to pray for a greater manifestation of His power upon the whole church of God. How much we have dishonored Him in the past! How ignorant we have been of His grace and love and presence! True, we have heard of Him and read of Him, but we have had little intelligent knowledge of His attributes, His offices, and His relations to us. I fear He has not been an actual presence in the lives of many professed Christians, nor is He known to them as a personality of the Godhead.

The first work of the Spirit is to give life—spiritual life. He gives it, and He sustains it. If there is no life, there can be no power. When the Spirit imparts this life, He does not leave us to droop and die but constantly fans the flame. He is ever with us. Surely we should not be ignorant of His power and His work.

Identity and Personality

In 1 John 5:7 we read:

There are three that bear record in heaven, the Father, the Word, and the Holy Ghost: and these three are one.

The Father is the first person of the Trinity; Christ, the Word, is the second; and the Holy Spirit, perfectly fulfilling His own office and work in union with the Father and the Son, is the third. The Bible clearly presents that the one God, who demands my love, service, and worship, has revealed Himself, and that each of those three names—Father, Son, and Holy Spirit—has personality attached to it. Therefore, we find some things ascribed to God as Father, some to God as Savior, and some to God as Comforter and Teacher.

It has been said that the Father plans, the Son executes, and the Holy Spirit applies. Such a distinction of persons is often noted in Scripture. In Matthew 3:13–17 we find Jesus submitting to baptism, the Spirit descending upon Him, and the Father's voice of approval saying, *This is my beloved Son, in whom I am well pleased* (v. 17).

In John 14:16 we read, *I [Jesus] will pray the Father, and he shall give you another Comforter.* Also, in Ephesians 2:18 we read, *Through him [Christ Jesus] we both [Jews and Gentiles] have access by one Spirit unto the Father.* From these and other Scriptures, we learn the identity and actual existence of the Holy Spirit, and we learn the distinction of persons in the Godhead. But I also believe that they plan and work together, for these Scriptures likewise reveal their inseparable union.

If you question whether I understand what is thus revealed in Scripture, I say no. But my faith bows down before the inspired Word, and I unhesitatingly believe the great things of God, even when reason is blinded and the intellect confused.

In addition to the teaching of God's Word, the Holy Spirit, in His gracious work in the soul, declares His own presence. The Holy Spirit, who inspired prophets and who qualified apostles, continues to animate, guide, and comfort all true believers. Through His agency we are born again, and through His indwelling we possess superhuman power. What has been falsely called *science,* when examined against the existence and presence of the Spirit of God with His people, only exposes its own folly, and those who have become new creatures in Christ Jesus (see 2 Corinthians 5:17) can only look on it with contempt.

To the true Christian, the personality of the Holy Spirit is more real than any theory that science has to offer, for so-called science is but mere calculation based on human observation and is constantly changing its inferences. But the existence of the Holy Spirit is, to the child of God, a matter of Scripture revelation and of actual experience.

Some skeptics assert that there is no other vital energy in the world but physical force, while, contrary to their assertions, thousands and tens of thousands who cannot possibly be deceived have been quickened into spiritual life by a power neither physical nor mental. Men who were dead in sins—drunkards who lost their will, blasphemers who lost their purity, libertines who were sunk in beastliness, infidels who published their shame to the world—have, in numberless instances, become the subjects of the Spirit's power. In fact, these men are now walking in the true nobility of Christian manhood, separated from their former lives by an infinite distance.

Let others reject this imperishable truth if they will, but they will do so to their own peril. I believe—and I am growing stronger in this belief—that divine, miraculous, creative power resides in the Holy Spirit. Above and beyond all natural law, yet in harmony with it, creation, providence, the divine government, and the upbuilding of the church of God are all presided over by the Spirit of God. His ministration is the ministration of life more glorious than the ministration of law. (See 2 Corinthians 3:6–10.) And, like the eternal Son, the eternal Spirit, having life in Himself (see John 5:26), is working out *all things after the counsel of his own will*" (Eph. 1:11) and for the everlasting glory of the triune Godhead.

The Holy Spirit has all the qualities belonging to a person: the power to understand, to will, to do, to call, to feel, to love. This cannot be said of a mere influence. The Holy Spirit possesses attributes and qualities that can only be ascribed to a person; indeed, acts and deeds are performed by Him that cannot be performed by a machine, an influence, or a result.

Emblems of the Spirit

Just as a balance is an emblem of justice, a crown an emblem of royalty, and a scepter an emblem of power, the emblems of the Holy Spirit reveal His character to us. In Exodus 17:6 we find that water is an emblem of the Spirit:

> *Behold, I will stand before thee there upon the rock in Horeb; and thou shalt smite the rock, and there shall come water out of it, that the people may drink. And Moses did so in the sight of the elders of Israel.*

The work of the Trinity is illustrated here in the smitten rock in the wilderness. How can this be?

In 1 Corinthians, Paul declared that the rock was Christ; it represented Christ. (See 1 Corinthians 10:1–4.) God said, in the above passage from Exodus, *"I will stand...upon the rock,"* and as Moses smote the rock, the water came out. It was an emblem of the Holy Spirit. It flowed out through the camp, and they drank of the water. Now, water is cleansing; it is fertilizing; it is refreshing; it is abundant; and it is freely given. The Spirit of God is the same: cleansing, fertilizing, refreshing, reviving, and freely given when the smitten Christ was glorified.

Fire is also an emblem of the Spirit (see Acts 2:1, 3–4): it is purifying, illuminating, searching. We talk about searching our hearts. We cannot do it. What we need is to have God search them. Oh, that God may search us and bring out the hidden things, the secret things, that cluster there, and bring them to light! (See Psalm 139:23.)

The wind is another emblem. (See Acts 2:2.) It is independent, powerful, perceptible in its effects, and reviving. How the Spirit of God revives when He comes to all the languished and weary members of the church! Other emblems are the rain and the dew (Ps. 72:6–7; Hos. 14:5–7): fertilizing, refreshing, abundant; the dove (Luke 3:22): gentle—what is more gentle than the dove?—and the lamb: gentle, meek, innocent, a sacrifice. (See Galatians 5:22–23.)

We read of the wrath of God; we read of the wrath of the Lamb (Rev. 6:16); but nowhere do we read of the wrath of the Holy Spirit. He is gentle, innocent, meek, loving; and that Spirit wants to take possession of our hearts. He comes as a voice, another emblem (see Luke 3:22; 2 Peter 1:17–18): speaking, guiding, warning, teaching; and as a seal (see Ephesians 1:13): impressing, securing, and making us His own.

Agent and Instrument

The Holy Spirit is closely identified with these words of the Lord Jesus:

It is the spirit that quickeneth; the flesh profiteth nothing: the words that I speak

unto you, they are spirit, and they are life.
(John 6:63)

Clearly the gospel proclamation cannot be divorced from the Holy Spirit. Unless He attends the Word in power, any attempt to preach it will be in vain. Human eloquence and persuasiveness of speech become like trappings of the dead, if the living Spirit is absent from them; the prophet may preach to the bones in the valley, but it must be the breath from heaven that will cause the slain to live. (See Ezekiel 37:1–10.)

In the third chapter of 1 Peter we read:

For Christ also hath once suffered for sins, the just for the unjust, that he might bring us to God, being put to death in the flesh, but quickened by the Spirit. (1 Pet. 3:18)

Here we see that Christ was raised up from the grave by the Spirit, and the power exercised to raise Christ's dead body must raise our dead souls and quicken them. No other power on earth can quicken a dead soul except the power that raised the body of Jesus Christ out of Joseph's sepulchre. And, if we want that power to quicken our friends who are dead in sin, we must look to God, and not to man, to do it. If we look alone to ministers, if we look alone to Christ's disciples to do this work, we will be disappointed; but if we look to the Spirit of God and expect it to come from Him and Him alone, then we will honor the Spirit, and the Spirit will do His work.

The Secret of Efficiency

I cannot help but believe that there are many Christians who want to be more efficient in the Lord's service. But they must first see from whom they can expect this power. The aim of this book is to take up this subject of the Holy Spirit, that they may see and understand the secret of efficiency.

Some of the last words recorded in the gospel of Matthew begin, *"Go ye therefore, and teach all nations, baptizing them in the name of the Father, and of the Son, and of the Holy Ghost"* (Matt. 28:19). Here we find that the Holy Spirit and the Son are equal with the Father; they are one with Him. Christ was handing His commission over to His apostles. He was going to leave them; His work on earth was finished, and He was just about ready to take His seat at the right hand of God. He said to them, *"All power is given unto me in heaven and in earth"* (v. 18).

Notice that the Scripture says, *"all power."* Therefore, He had authority. If Christ were merely a man, as some people try to make Him out to be, it would have been blasphemy for Him to have said to the disciples, "Go, and baptize all nations in the name of the Father, and in My name, and in that of the Holy Spirit." He was making Himself equal with the Father.

There are three things that I want you to observe in these Scriptures. First, *"**All** power is given unto me"* (Matt. 28:18, emphasis added). Second, *"Go...teach **all** nations"* (v. 19, emphasis added). And, third, teach them what? *"To observe **all** things"* (v. 20, emphasis added). There are a great many people who are willing to observe what they like about Christ, but they just dismiss and turn away from the things that they don't like. But His commission to His disciples was, *"Go...teach all nations...to observe all things whatsoever I have commanded you"* (vv. 19–20).

Does a messenger, who has been sent by God, have any right to change the message? If I had sent a servant to deliver a message, and the servant thought the message didn't sound exactly right— maybe, in his eyes, it seemed a little harsh—and that servant went and changed the message, I would change servants very quickly; he could not serve me any longer. Likewise, when a minister or a messenger of Christ begins to change the message, because he thinks it is not exactly what it should be and he thinks he is wiser than God, God just dismisses that man.

So many of our pastors and ministers have not taught *"all things."* They have left out some of the things that Christ has commanded us to teach, because these things didn't correspond with man's reason. However, we have to take the Word of God just as it is; we have no authority to take from it only what we like, or only what we think is appropriate, and to let dark reason be our guide. Rather, we are to let the Holy Spirit be our guide.

It is the work of the Spirit to impress the heart and seal the preached Word. His office is to take of the things of Christ and reveal them to us. (See John 16:13–15.)

Some people have the idea that this is the only function of the Holy Spirit, that He didn't work until Christ was glorified. But Simeon felt the Holy Spirit when he went into the temple. (See Luke 2:25–27.) Then, in 2 Peter 1:21, we read, *Holy men of God spake as they were moved by the Holy Ghost.* We find the same Spirit in Genesis as is seen in Revelation. The same Spirit that guided the hand that wrote Exodus also inspired the Epistles, and we find the same Spirit speaking from one end of the Bible to the other. So, holy men in all ages have spoken as they were moved by the Holy Spirit.

His Personality

I was a Christian for a long time before I found out that the Holy Spirit was a person. Now, this is something a great many people don't seem to understand. However, if you will just take up the Bible and see what Christ had to say about the Holy Spirit, you will find that Christ always spoke of Him as a person—He never spoke of Him as an influence.

Some people have the idea that the Holy Spirit is an attribute of God, just as mercy is an attribute of God. They think of the Spirit as just an influence coming from God. But we find these words in the fourteenth chapter of John: *"And I will pray the Father, and he shall give you another Comforter, that he may abide with you for ever"* (v. 16). Note that it says, *"That **he** may abide with you for ever."* And the following verse reads:

> *Even the Spirit of truth; whom the world cannot receive, because it seeth him not, neither knoweth him: but ye know him; for he dwelleth with you, and shall be in you.*   (John 14:17)

Again, in the twenty-sixth verse of the same chapter, we find:

> *But the Comforter, which is the Holy Ghost, whom the Father will send in my name, he shall teach you all things, and bring all things to your remembrance, whatsoever I have said unto you.*

Observe the pronouns *"he"* and *"him."* I want to call attention to this fact, that whenever Christ spoke of the Holy Spirit, He spoke of Him as a person, not as mere influence. If we want to honor the Holy Spirit, let us bear in mind that He is one of the Trinity, a personality of the Godhead.

The Reservoir of Love

We read that *"the fruit of the Spirit is love"* (Gal. 5:22). We also know from the Scriptures that *"God is love"* (1 John 4:8, 16) and that Christ is love. Therefore, we should not be surprised to read about the love of the Spirit. What a blessed attribute this is! Let us call it the dome of the temple of the graces. Better still, it is the crown of crowns, worn by the triune God.

Human love is a natural emotion that flows forth toward the object of our affections. But divine love is as high above human love as heaven is above the earth. The natural man is of the earth—that is, earthly—and however pure his love may be, it is weak and imperfect at best. But the love of God is perfect and entire, lacking nothing. It is as a mighty ocean in its greatness, dwelling with and flowing from the eternal Spirit. In Romans 5:5 we read:

> *And hope maketh not ashamed; because the love of God is shed abroad in our hearts by the Holy Ghost which is given unto us.*

Now, if we are coworkers with God, there is one thing we must possess, and that is love. A lawyer may have no love for his clients and yet be very successful and get on very well. A physician may have no love for his patients and yet be a very successful, good physician. A merchant may have no love for his customers and yet be very successful and run a prosperous business. But no man can be a coworker with God without love. If our service is a mere profession on our part, the more quickly we renounce it, the better. If a man takes up God's work as he would take up any profession, the sooner he gets out of it, the better.

We cannot work for God without love. Love is the only tree that can produce fruit that is acceptable to God on this sin-cursed earth. If I have no love for God or for my fellowman, then I cannot work acceptably. *"I am become as sounding brass, or a tinkling cymbal"* (1 Cor. 13:1). We are told that *"the love of God is shed abroad in our hearts by the Holy Ghost"* (Rom. 5:5). Now, if we have had that love put into our hearts, then we are ready for God's service; if we have not, we are not ready. It is so easy to reach a man when you love him; all barriers are broken down and swept away.

Paul, when writing to Titus, told him to be sound in faith, in charity, and in patience. (See Titus 2:1–2.) Now, in this age, ever since I can remember, the church has been very intolerant of men who show signs of being unsound in the faith. If a man becomes unsound in the faith, people in the church draw their ecclesiastical swords and cut at him; but he may be ever so unsound in love, and they don't say anything. He may be ever so defective in patience, he may be irritable and fretful all the time, but they never deal with him.

Now, the Bible teaches us that we are to be sound not only in the faith, but also in love and in patience. I believe God cannot use many of His servants, because they are full of irritability and impatience; they are fretting all the time, from morning until night. God cannot use them; their mouths are sealed; they cannot speak for Jesus Christ, and if they do not have any love, they cannot work for God.

I do not mean love for those who love us; it doesn't take grace to do that. The rudest Hottentot in the world can do that; the greatest heathen that ever lived can do that; the vilest man that ever walked the earth can do that. It doesn't take any grace at all. I did that before I ever became a Christian. Love begets love; hatred begets hatred. If I know a man loves me first, my love will naturally go out toward him. But it requires the grace of God to love the man who hates me. (See Luke 6:32–35.)

Suppose a man comes to me, saying, "Mr. Moody, a certain man told me today that he thinks you are the meanest man alive." Well, if I didn't have a good deal of the grace of God in my heart, then I know there would be hard feelings that would spring up in my heart against that man, and it would not be long before I would be talking against him. Hatred begets hatred.

But suppose a man comes to me and says, "Mr. Moody, do you know that a man whom I met today says that he thinks a great deal of you?" Though I may never have heard of him, there would be love for him springing up in my heart. Love begets love; we all know that. But it takes the grace of God to love the man who lies about me, the man who slanders me, the man who tears down my character; it takes the grace of God to love that man. You may hate the sin he has committed (there is a difference between the sin and the sinner), you may hate the sin with a perfect hatred, but you must love the sinner. You cannot otherwise do him any good.

The Right Overflow

Now, you know the first impulse of a young convert is to love. Do you remember the day you were converted? Was your heart not full of sweet peace and love?

I remember the morning I came out of my room after I had first trusted Christ, and I thought the sun shone a good deal brighter than it ever had before. I thought that the sun was just smiling upon me as I walked out upon Boston Common. I heard the birds in the trees, and I thought that they were all singing a song for me. Do you know, I fell in love with the birds? I never cared for them before, yet it seemed to me that I was now in love with all creation. I did not have a bitter feeling against any man, and I was ready to take all men to my heart.

If a man does not have the love of God in his heart, you may be assured that he has never been regenerated. If a person gets up in a prayer meeting and begins to speak and find fault with everyone, you may know that his is not a genuine conversion. Rather, it is counterfeit; it does not have the right ring, because the impulse of a converted soul is to love and not to be getting up and complaining about and finding fault with everyone else.

But it is hard for us to live in the right atmosphere all the time. Perhaps when someone comes along and treats us wrongly, we hate him; if so, we have not attended to the means of grace and have not kept feeding on the Word of God as we should. A root of bitterness springs up in our hearts (Heb. 12:15); perhaps we are not aware of it, but it has come up in our hearts. Then we are not satisfied to work for God. The love of God is not shed abroad in our hearts by the Holy Spirit as it ought to be.

But the work of the Holy Spirit is to impart love. Paul said, *"The love of Christ constraineth* [me]" (2 Cor. 5:14), because he could not help going from town to town and preaching the Gospel. Jeremiah at one time said, "I will speak no more in the Lord's name; I have suffered enough; these people don't like God's Word." (See Jeremiah 20:8–9.) Jeremiah lived in a wicked day, as we do now. Infidels were creeping up all around him, saying that the Word of God was not true; but Jeremiah stood like a wall of fire, confronting them, and he boldly proclaimed that the Word of God was true. At last they put him in prison (see Jeremiah 32:2), and he said, "I will keep still; it has cost me too much." But he could not keep still. His bones caught fire; he had to speak. (See Jeremiah 20:9.)

When we are as full of the love of God as Jeremiah was, we are compelled to work for God, and then God blesses us. On the other hand, if our work is accomplished without any true motive power, perhaps because we feel obliged to do it, it will come to nothing.

Now the question comes up, do we have the love of God shed abroad in our hearts, and are we holding the truth in love? Some people hold the truth, but in such a cold, stern way that it will do no good. Other people want to love everything, and so they give up much of the truth. But we are to hold the truth in love. We are to hold the truth even if we lose all, but we are to hold it in love; and if we do that, the Lord will bless us.

Many people are trying to get this love; they are trying to produce it of themselves. But therein all fail. The love implanted deep in our new nature will be spontaneous. It will be like loving one's own children. I don't have to learn to love my children; I cannot help loving them.

Some time ago, I met a young woman who said that she could not love God, that it was very hard for her to love Him. I said to her, "Is it hard for you to love your mother? Do you have to learn to love your mother?"

She looked up through her tears and said, "No, I can't help it; that is spontaneous."

26

"Well," I said, "when the Holy Spirit kindles love in your heart, you cannot help loving God; it will be spontaneous." When the Spirit of God comes into your heart and mine, it will be easy to serve God.

The fruit of the Spirit, as you find it in Galatians, begins with love. (See Galatians 5:22–23.) There are nine graces spoken of here, and of the nine different graces, Paul put love at the head of the list. Love is the first thing, the first in that precious cluster of fruit. Someone has said that all the other eight can be included in the word *love*. Joy is love exulting; peace is love in repose; long-suffering is love on trial; gentleness is love in society; goodness is love in action; faith is love on the battlefield; meekness is love at school; and temperance is love in training.

Love is at the top, at the bottom, and all the way through these graces; and if we only brought forth the fruit of the Spirit, what a world we would have! There would be no need for any policemen; a man could leave his overcoat around without someone stealing it; men would not have any desire to do evil. As Paul said, *"Against such there is no law"* (Gal. 5:23); in other words, we wouldn't need any law. A man who is full of the Spirit doesn't need to be put under law; he doesn't need any policemen to watch him. We could dismiss all our policemen, the lawyers would have to give up practicing law, and the courts would not have any business.

The Triumphs of Hope

In the fifteenth chapter of Romans the apostle wrote:

Now the God of hope fill you with all joy and peace in believing, that ye may abound in hope, through the power of the Holy Ghost. (v. 13)

The next thing, then, is hope.

Did you ever notice that no man or woman who has lost hope is ever used by God to build up His kingdom? I have been observing this throughout different parts of the country, and, wherever I have found a worker in God's vineyard who has lost hope, I have found a man or woman who is not very useful.

Now, look at these workers. Let your mind go over the past for a moment. Can you think of a man or woman who has lost hope, whom God has used to build His kingdom? I don't know of any; I never heard of such a person. It is very important that believers have hope, and it is the work of the Holy Spirit to impart hope. Let Him come into some of the churches where there have not been any conversions for a few years, and let Him convert a score of people, and the church will become hopeful at once, for the Spirit imparts hope. A man who is filled with the Spirit of God will be very hopeful; he will be looking out into the future, and he will know that it is all bright, because the God of all grace is able to do great things. Therefore, it is very important that we have hope.

If a man has lost hope, he is out of communion with God; he does not have the Spirit of God resting upon him for service. He may be a son of God, but he is so disheartened that he cannot be used of God. There is no place in the Scriptures where it is recorded that God ever used even a discouraged man.

Some years ago, I was quite discouraged in my work, and I was ready to hang my harp on the willow. (See Psalm 137:2.) I was depressed a great deal. I had been in that state for weeks, when one morning a friend, who had a very large Bible class, came into my study. I used to examine the notes of his Sunday school lessons, which were equal to sermons, and he came to me that morning and asked, "What did you preach about yesterday?" and I told him.

Then I said, "What did you preach about?" and he said that he had preached about Noah. "Did you ever preach about Noah?" he asked.

"No, I never preached about Noah."

"Did you ever study his character?"

"No, I never studied his life particularly."

"Well," said he, "he is a most wonderful character. It will do you good. You ought to study up that character."

When he went out, I opened my Bible and read about Noah; and then it came over me that Noah worked a hundred and twenty years and never had a single convert, and yet he did not get discouraged. So I said to myself, "Well, I should not be discouraged," and I closed my Bible, got up, and walked downtown. The cloud over my spirit had gone.

I went down to the noon prayer meeting, and there I heard of a little town in the country where they had taken into the church a hundred young converts. I asked myself, "What would Noah have given if he could have heard that?" And yet he worked a hundred and twenty years and didn't get discouraged.

Just then, a man right across the aisle got up and said, "My friends, I wish you to pray for me; I think I'm lost." And I thought to myself, "I wonder what Noah would have given to hear that." He never heard a man say, "I wish you to pray for me; I think I am lost," and yet he didn't get discouraged!

It does me good sometimes to meet people who are very hopeful. Other people throw a gloom over me because they are cast down all the time, looking at the dark side and at the obstacles and difficulties that are in the way. Oh, children of God, let us not get discouraged; let us ask God to forgive us if we have been discouraged and cast down; let us ask God to give us hope through His Holy Spirit, that we may be ever hopeful and that we may have power for His service.

The Boon of Liberty

The next thing the Spirit of God does is to give us liberty. He first imparts love; He next inspires hope; and He then gives liberty, and that is a very rare thing in many of our churches today. I am sorry to say there must be a funeral in a good many churches before any work can be done. Indeed, we have to bury the formalism so deep that it will never have any resurrection.

The last thing to be found in many churches is liberty. When the Gospel happens to be preached, the churchgoers criticize it, just as they would a theatrical performance. It is exactly the same to them, and many professed Christians never think of listening to what the man of God, speaking from the pulpit, actually has to say. It is hard work to preach to carnally minded critics, but, *"where the Spirit of the Lord is, there is liberty"* (2 Cor. 3:17).

Very often, a churchgoer will hear a hundred good things in a sermon, but the one thing that strikes him as a little out of place will disturb him so much that he will go home and talk about it right in front of his children. He will magnify that one wrong thing, but he won't say a word about the hundred good things that were said. That is what people do who criticize.

There are so many people who, the moment you talk to them and insinuate that they are not doing what good they could be doing, will say, "I have life. I am a Christian." Well, they may say so, but, in actuality, they are bound hand and foot. God does not use men in captivity. The condition of many is like Lazarus when he came out of the sepulchre, *"bound hand and foot"* (John 11:44). The bandage had not yet been taken off his mouth, and he could not speak. He had life, and if you had said Lazarus was not alive, you would have told a falsehood, because he was raised from the dead. But he was still bound, just as many people are today.

May God snap these fetters and set His children free, that they may have liberty! I believe He comes to set us free, and wants us to work for Him and speak for Him. How many people would like to get up in a social prayer meeting to say a few words for Christ, but there is such a cold spirit of criticism in the church that they dare not do it? They do not have the liberty to do it. If they get up, they are so frightened by these critics that they begin to tremble, and so they sit down. They cannot say anything. And so many people go to the prayer meeting out of a cold sense of duty. They think, "I must attend because I feel it is my duty." They don't think it is a glorious privilege to meet and pray, to be strengthened, and to help someone else in the wilderness journey.

Now, that is all wrong. The Spirit of God comes to give liberty, and wherever you see the Lord's work going on, you will see that Spirit of liberty. People won't be afraid to speak to one another. And when the meeting is over, they will not get their coats and see how quickly they can get out of the church, but they will begin to shake hands with one another, and there will be liberty there.

What we need today is love in our hearts. Don't we want it? Don't we want hope in our lives? Don't we want to be hopeful? Don't we want liberty? Now, all this is the work of the Spirit of God, and so we ought to pray daily, asking God to give us love, hope, and liberty. We read in Hebrews, *"Having therefore, brethren, boldness to enter into the holiest by the blood of Jesus"* (Heb. 10:19). This passage has also been translated, "Having, therefore, brethren, liberty to enter into the holiest." We can go into the Holy of Holies, having freedom of access, and plead for this love and liberty and glorious hope, that we may not rest until God, through His Spirit, gives us the power to work for Him.

If I know my own heart today, I would rather die than live as I once did, a mere nominal Christian, not used by God in building up His kingdom. It seems a poor, empty life to live for the sake of self.

Let us seek to be useful. Let us seek to be vessels fit for the Master's use (see 2 Timothy 2:21) so that God the Holy Spirit may shine fully through us.

Chapter Two

Power in Operation

Chapter Two

Power in Operation

The power we have been considering is the presence of the Holy Spirit. We will now consider how this power is manifested in the Christian life. Power in operation is the action of the Spirit, or the fruit of the Spirit. What is meant by this? Paul wrote in Galatians 5,

> *This I say then, Walk in the Spirit, and ye shall not fulfil the lust of the flesh. For the flesh lusteth against the Spirit, and the Spirit against the flesh: and these are contrary, the one to the other: so that ye cannot do the things that ye would. But if ye be led of the Spirit, ye are not under the law....But the fruit of the Spirit is love, joy, peace, longsuffering, gentleness, goodness, faith, meekness, temperance: against such there is no law. And they that are Christ's*

have crucified the flesh with the affections and lusts. If we live in the Spirit, let us also walk in the Spirit. Let us not be desirous of vain glory, provoking one another, envying one another.
(Gal. 5:16–18, 22–26)

Now, there is a life of perfect peace, perfect joy, and perfect love that ought to be the aim of every child of God. Such should be the standard for Christians, and they should not rest until they have attained that position. That is God's standard, where He wants all His children.

The nine graces given in Galatians 5 can be divided in this way: Love, peace, and joy are all related to God. God looks for these three fruits from each one of His children, and that is the kind of fruit that is acceptable to Him. Without that, we cannot please God. He wants—above everything else that we possess—love, peace, and joy. And then the next three, goodness, long-suffering, and gentleness, are toward man. These are part of our outward lives to those whom we are coming in contact with continually, every day, and even by the hour. The next three, faith, temperance, and meekness, are in relation to ourselves. Our study in this chapter will focus on the first division of the fruit of the Spirit.

The First Three Graces

The first thing that meets us as we enter the kingdom of God, you might say, are these first three graces, love, peace, and joy. When a man who has been living in sin turns from his sins and turns to God with all his heart, he is met on the threshold of the divine life by these sister graces. The love of God is shed abroad in his heart by the Holy Spirit (Rom. 5:5). The peace of God comes at the same time, and also the joy of the Lord.

We can all test ourselves to see if we have love, peace, and joy. They are not anything that we can fabricate. The great trouble with many people is that they are trying to make these graces. They are trying to manufacture love; they are trying to produce peace; they are trying to make joy. But such graces are not creatures of human planting. To produce them of ourselves is impossible. That is an act of God. They come from above. It is God who speaks the word and gives the love; it is God who gives the peace; it is God who gives the joy. We can only possess these by receiving Jesus Christ by faith into our hearts; for when Christ comes by faith into the heart, then the Spirit is there, and if we have the Spirit, we will have the fruit.

If the whole church of God could live as the Lord would have them live, Christianity would be the mightiest power this world has ever seen. It is the low standard of Christian life that is causing so much trouble. There are a great many stunted Christians in the church. Their lives are stunted; they are like trees planted in poor soil: the soil is hard and stony, and the roots cannot find the rich, loamy soil needed for growth. Such believers have not grown in these sweet graces. Peter, in his second epistle, wrote:

And beside this, giving all diligence, add to your faith virtue; and to virtue knowledge; and to knowledge temperance; and to temperance patience; and to patience godliness; and to god-liness brotherly kindness; and to brotherly kind-ness charity. For if these things be in you, and abound, they make you that ye shall neither be barren nor unfruitful in the knowledge of our Lord Jesus Christ. (2 Pet. 1:5–8)

Now, if we have these things in us, I believe that we will be constantly bringing forth fruit that will be acceptable to God. It won't be just a little every now and then, when we work ourselves up into a certain state of mind or into an excited con-dition. We will not just work a little while and then become cold and discouraged and disheartened; we will be neither unfruitful nor barren, bringing forth fruit constantly; we will grow in grace and be filled with the Spirit of God.

What Wins

A great many parents have inquired of me how to win their children. They say they have talked with them, and sometimes they have scolded them and lectured them, and they have failed consider-ably. I think there is no way so sure to win our fami-lies and our neighbors to Christ, and those about whom we are anxious than to adorn the doctrine of Jesus Christ in our lives and to grow in all these graces. If we have peace and joy and love and gentleness and goodness and temperance; if we are not only temperate in what we drink but also in what we eat; if we are temperate in our language and guarded in our expressions; if we live in our homes as the Lord would have us live; if we live an uncompromising Christian life, day by day, we will have a quiet and silent power proceeding from us—a power that will certainly bring them to believe in the Lord Jesus Christ.

But an uneven life, hot today and cold tomorrow, will only repel them. Many are watching God's people. It is a terrible thing when those whom we want to win to Christ see us, at any time, in a cold, backslidden state. This is not the normal condition of the church; it is not God's intention. He would have us growing in all these graces, and the only true, happy, Christian life is to be growing, constantly growing, in the love and favor of God, growing in all those delightful graces of the Spirit.

Even the vilest, the most impure, acknowledge the power of goodness; they recognize the fruit of the Spirit. It may condemn their lives and cause them to say bitter things at times, but deep down in their hearts they know that the man or woman who is living that kind of life is superior to them. The world doesn't satisfy them, and if we can show the world that Jesus Christ does satisfy us in our present life, it will be more powerful than the most eloquent words of professional reformers.

A man may preach with the eloquence of an angel, but if he doesn't live what he preaches and act out in his home and his business what he professes, his testimony is worth nothing. The people will say it is all hypocrisy; it is all a sham. Words are empty if there is no substance behind them. Your testimony is poor and worthless if the record of your life is not consistent with what you profess. What we need is to pray to God to lift us up out of this low, cold, formal state that we have been living in so that we may live in the atmosphere of God continually, that the Lord may lift up the light of His countenance upon us (see Psalm 4:6), and that we may shine in this world, reflecting His grace and glory. (See Matthew 5:16; Philippians 2:15.)

Love's Power

The first of the graces spoken of in Galatians, and the last mentioned in 2 Peter, is charity, or love. We cannot serve God, we cannot work for God, unless we have love. That is the key that unlocks the human heart. If I can prove to a man that I come to him out of pure love, his heart will soon be open to the Word of God. If a mother shows by her actions that it is pure love, not a selfish love, that prompts her to advise her boy to lead a different life, one that is for the glory of God, it won't be long before that mother's influence will be felt by the boy, and he will begin to think about this matter. This happens because true love touches the heart more quickly than anything else.

Love is the badge that Christ gave His disciples. These days, some people put on one sort of badge and some another. Some put on a strange kind of dress, that they may be known as Christians, and some wear a crucifix, or something else, that they may be known as Christians. But love is the only badge by which the disciples of our Lord Jesus Christ are known. *"By this shall all men know that ye are my disciples, if ye have love one to another"* (John 13:35).

Therefore, though a man stand before an audience and speak with the eloquence of a Demosthenes,[1] or of the greatest living orator, if there is no love in his words, it is like *"sounding brass, or a tinkling cymbal"* (1 Cor. 13:1). I recommend that all Christians read the thirteenth chapter of 1 Corinthians constantly, abiding in it day and night, not spending a night or a day reading it, but spending all their time—summer and winter, twelve months in the year—meditating upon it. Then the power of Christ and Christianity would be felt as it never has been in the history of the world.

See what 1 Corinthians 13 says at its very beginning:

---

[1] Demosthenes (384–322 B.C.): an Athenian orator and statesman.

Though I speak with the tongues of men and of angels, and have not charity, I am become as sounding brass, or a tinkling cymbal. And though I have the gift of prophecy, and understand all mysteries, and all knowledge; and though I have all faith, so that I could remove mountains, and have not charity, I am nothing. (1 Cor. 13:1–2)

A great many Christians are praying for faith. They want extraordinary faith, they want remarkable faith, but they forget that love exceeds faith.

The charity spoken of in the above verses is love, the fruit of the Spirit, the great motive power of life. What the church of God needs today is love: more love for God and more love for our fellowman. If we love God more, we will love our fellowman more. There is no doubt about that.

I used to think that I would have liked living in the days of the prophets. I thought I would have liked being one of the prophets, prophesying and seeing the beauties of heaven, then describing them to men. However, as I understand the Scriptures now, I would rather live in the thirteenth chapter of 1 Corinthians and have this love that Paul wrote about—the love of God burning in my soul like an unquenchable flame—so that I may reach men and win them for heaven.

A man may have wonderful knowledge, such that may unravel the mysteries of the Bible, and yet he may be as cold as an icicle. He may glisten like the snow in the sun. You may have wondered why it is that certain ministers, who have such wonderful magnetism, who have such a marvelous command of language, and who preach with such mental strength, haven't had more conversions. If the truth were known, I believe you would find no divine love behind their words, no pure love in their sermons.

Let us further examine this passage in 1 Corinthians 13. You may preach like an angel, Paul said, *"with the tongues of men and of angels"* (v. 1), but if you do not have love, it amounts to nothing. *"And though* [you] *bestow all* [your] *goods to feed the poor"* (v. 3)—though a man may be very charitable and give away all his goods, though he may give all that he has—if it is not the love of God that prompts the gift, it will not be acceptable to God. *"And though I give my body to be burned, and have not charity* [that is, have not love], *it profiteth me nothing"* (v. 3). A man may go to the stake for his principles, he may go to the stake for what he believes, but if it is not love for God that actuates him, then it will not be acceptable to God.

Love's Wonderful Effects

Charity suffereth long, and is kind; charity envieth not; charity vaunteth not itself, is not puffed up, doth not behave itself unseemly, seeketh not her own, is not easily provoked, thinketh no evil.   (1 Cor. 13:4–5)

That is the work of love. It is not easily provoked. Now, if a man has no love for God in his
heart, it is quite easy for him to become offended;
he may perhaps become offended by the church
because some members don't treat him just right or
because some men of the church don't shake hands
with him when they happen to meet him in public.
He takes offense, and that is the last you see of
him.

But love is long-suffering. If I love the Lord
Jesus Christ, these little things are not going to sep-
arate me from His people. They are like dust on a
balance, having almost no weight. Nor will the cold,
formal behavior of hypocrites in the church quench
the love that I have for Him in my heart. Indeed,
if this love is in the heart, and the fire is burning
on the altar, we will not be all the time finding fault
with other people and criticizing what they have
done.

Critics, Beware

The habit of finding fault constantly is very
damaging to spiritual life; it is about the lowest and
meanest position that a man can take. Love will
rebuke evil; it will not rejoice in it. Love will be
impatient with sin, but patient with the sinner. I
have never seen a man who was aiming to do
the best work who couldn't have benefited from
some kind of improvement. In fact, I have never
done anything in my own life that I didn't think I
could have done better, and I have often upbraided

myself for not doing better. But to sit down and find fault with other people, when we are doing nothing ourselves, when we are not lifting a finger to save someone, is all wrong, and it is the opposite of holy, patient, divine love.

Love is forbearance, and what we need is to get this spirit of criticism and faultfinding out of the church and out of our hearts. Each one of us ought to live as if we had to answer for ourselves, and not for the community, on the Last Day. If we are living according to the thirteenth chapter of 1 Corinthians, we will not be finding fault with other people all the time. Love *"suffereth long, and is kind"* (v. 4). Love forgets itself and doesn't dwell on itself.

The woman who came to Christ with that alabaster box (see Matthew 26:7), I venture to say, never thought of herself. Little did she know what an act she was performing. She was filled with love for the Master. She forgot the surroundings; she forgot everything else that was there. She broke that box and poured the ointment upon Him, filling the house with its fragrance. The act has been remembered for over nineteen hundred years. It is right here; the perfume of that box is in the world today.

That ointment was worth forty or fifty dollars—no small sum in those days for a poor woman. Judas sold the Son of God for about fifteen or twenty dollars. But what this woman gave to Christ was everything that she had, and she become so occupied with Jesus Christ that she didn't think about what people were going to say. So, when we act with our eyes focused on the glory of our Lord, not finding fault with everything around us, but doing what we can in the power of this love, then our deeds for God will speak, and the world will acknowledge that we have been with Jesus and that this glorious love has been *"shed abroad in our hearts"* (Rom. 5:5).

If we don't love the church of God, I am afraid it won't do us much good; if we don't love the blessed Bible, it will not do us much good. What we need, then, is to have love for Christ, to have love for His Word, and to have love for the church of God. Then, when we have love and are living in that spirit, we will not be in the spirit of finding fault and working mischief.

After Love, What?

After love comes peace. I remarked earlier that a great many people are trying to manufacture peace. But that has already been done. God has not left it for us to do. He has already made it; all that we have to do is enter into it. It is a condition that is already prepared for us, and instead of trying to make peace and to work for peace, we need to cease all that and sweetly enter into peace.

If I were to discover a man in the cellar, complaining because there is no light there and because it is cold and damp, I would say, "My friend, come up out of the cellar. The sun is shining; it is a beautiful spring day, and it is warm; it is cheerful and light. Come up, and enjoy it." Would he reply, "Oh, no, sir. I am trying to see if I can make light down here; I am trying to work myself into a warm feeling"? And yet, there he is, working away—and he has been at it for a whole week.

I can imagine my reader will smile at this; but you may be smiling at a portrayal of your own life, for this is the condition of many whom I meet every day, who are trying to do this very thing—they are trying to work themselves into peace and joyful feelings. Peace is a condition into which we enter. It is a state, and instead of trying to make peace, let us believe what God's Word declares: that peace has already been made by the blood of the cross (Col. 1:20). Christ has made peace for us, and now what He desires is that we believe it and enter into it.

Now, the only thing that can keep us from peace is sin. *"But the way of the wicked* [God] *turneth upside down"* (Ps. 146:9). *"There is no peace...unto the wicked"* (Isa. 48:22), says my God. They are *"like the troubled sea, when it cannot rest,"* casting up filth and mire all the while (Isa. 57:20). But peace with God by faith in Jesus Christ (see Romans 5:1)—peace through the knowledge of forgiven sin—is like a rock: the waters go dashing and surging past it, but it abides. When we find peace, we will not find it on the ground of innate goodness;

it comes from outside ourselves and flows into us. In John 16:33 we read Christ's words to us: *"These things I have spoken unto you, that in me ye might have peace."*

"In me ye might have peace." Jesus Christ is the Author of peace. He procured peace. His Gospel is the Gospel of peace. Recall what the angel said to the shepherds on the night of Christ's birth:

> *Behold, I bring you good tidings of great joy, which shall be unto all people. For unto you is born this day in the city of David a Saviour, which is Christ the Lord.* (Luke 2:10–11)

And then came that chorus from heaven: *"Glory to God in the highest, and on earth peace"* (v. 14). He brought peace. He says to us, *"In the world ye shall have tribulation: but be of good cheer; I have overcome the world"* (John 16:33).

How true that in the world we have tribulation. Are you in tribulation? Are you in trouble? Are you in sorrow? Remember, this is our lot. Paul had tribulation, and others shared in grief. We will not be exempt from trial. But, within us, peace may reign undisturbed. If sorrow is our lot, then peace is our legacy. Jesus gives peace, and do you know there is a good deal of difference between His peace and our peace? Anyone can disturb our peace, but they can't disturb His peace. That is the kind of peace He has left us. Nothing can offend those who trust in Christ.

Not Easily Offended

In Psalm 119:165 we find, *"Great peace have they which love thy law: and nothing shall offend them."* The study of God's Word will secure peace for us. If you observe those Christians who are rooted and grounded in the Word of God, you will find that they have great peace. But it is those who don't study their Bible, who don't know their Bible, who are easily offended when some little trouble comes—it is these whose peace is all disturbed; just a little breath of opposition, and their peace is all gone.

Sometimes I am amazed to see how little it takes to drive all peace and comfort from some people. A slandering tongue can easily blast it. But if we have the peace of God, the world cannot take that from us. The world cannot give it; the world cannot destroy it. We have to get this peace from above the world; it is the peace that Christ gives. (See John 14:27.) Remember, *"Great peace have they which love thy law: and nothing shall offend them"* (Ps. 119:165). Christ says, *"Blessed is he, whosoever shall not be offended in me"* (Matt. 11:6).

Now, if you will notice, wherever there is a Bible-taught Christian, one who has the Bible well marked and who daily feeds upon the Word by prayerful meditation, he will not be easily offended. Such are the people who are growing and working all the while. On the other hand, it is these people who never open their Bibles, these people who never study the Scriptures, who become offended and are wondering why they are having such a hard time. They are the people who tell you that Christianity is not what it was when they were first told about it, that they have found it was not all that we claim it to be.

The real trouble is that these people have not done as the Lord has told them to do. They have neglected the Word of God. If they had been studying the Word of God all along, they would not have wandered these years away from God, living on the husks of the world. But the trouble is, they have neglected to care for the new life; they haven't fed it, and the soul, being starved, has sunk into weakness and decay and is easily stumbled or offended.

I once met a man who confessed his soul had fed on nothing for forty years. "Well," I said, "that is pretty hard for the soul—giving it nothing to feed on!" Yet that man is but a type of thousands and tens of thousands today; their poor souls are starving. We take good care of this body that we inhabit for only a short time. We feed it three times a day; we clothe it and take care of it and decorate it; and by and by it is going into the grave to be eaten up by the worms. But the inner man, which is to live on and on and on, until forever, is lean and starved.

Sweet Words

In the sixth chapter of Numbers we read:

*And the LORD spake unto Moses, saying, Speak
unto Aaron and unto his sons, saying, On this
wise ye shall bless the children of Israel, saying
unto them, The LORD bless thee, and keep thee:
the LORD make his face shine upon thee, and
be gracious unto thee: the LORD lift up his
countenance upon thee, and give thee peace.*

(vv. 22–26)

I think these words are some of the sweetest we
will find in the Old Testament. I marked them
years ago in my Bible, and many times I have gone
back to read them. *"The LORD lift up his countenance
upon thee, and give thee peace."* They remind us of
the loving words of Jesus to His troubled disciples,
when He calmed the storm: *"Peace, be still"* (Mark
4:39). The Jewish salutation used to be, as a man
went into a house, "Peace be upon this house."
As he left the house, the host would say, "Go in
peace."

In the fourteenth chapter of John, in verse
twenty-seven, we find Jesus saying:

*Peace I leave with you, my peace I give unto
you: not as the world giveth, give I unto you.
Let not your heart be troubled, neither let it be
afraid.*

This is the precious legacy of Jesus to all His fol-
lowers. Every man, every woman, every child who
believes in Him, may share in this portion. Christ
has willed it to them, and His peace is theirs. This,

then, is our Lord's purpose and promise: *"'My peace I give unto you.' I give it, and I am not going to take it away again; I am going to leave it with you. 'Not as the world giveth, give I unto you. Let not your heart be troubled, neither let it be afraid.'"*

You know that, when some men make their wills and deed away their property, there are some sharp, shrewd lawyers who will get hold of that will and break it all to pieces. They will go into court and make the will seem worthless. The jury will set the will aside, and the money will go into another channel.

In contrast, neither devil nor man can break the will that Christ has made. He has promised to give us peace, and there are thousands of witnesses who can say, "I have my part of that legacy. I have peace; I came to Him for peace, and I got it. I came to Him in darkness; I came to Him in trouble and sorrow; I was passing under a deep cloud of affliction; and I came to Him and He said, *'Peace, be still'* (Mark 4:39). And from that hour, peace reigned in my soul."

Yes, many have proven the invitation true, *"Come unto me, all ye that labour and are heavy laden, and I will give you rest"* (Matt. 11:28). They found rest when they came. He is the Author of rest; He is the Author of peace, and no power can break that will. It is true that unbelief may question it, but Jesus Christ rose again to execute His own will; it is in vain for man to contest it. Infidels and skeptics may tell us that it is all a myth and that there isn't anything in it, and yet the glorious tidings are ever repeated, *"On earth peace, good will toward men"* (Luke 2:14). And the poor and needy, the sad and sorrowful, are made partakers of it.

So, my reader, you need not wait for peace any longer. All you have to do is enter into it today. You need not try to make peace. It is a false idea; you cannot make it. Peace is already made by Jesus Christ and is now declared unto you.

Peace Declared

When France and England were at war, a French vessel had gone off on a long voyage, a whaling voyage; and when it came back, the crew was short of water. Being near an English port, they wanted to get water, but they were afraid that they would be taken captive if they went into that port. Some people in the port saw them, saw their signal of distress, and sent word to them that they need not be afraid, that the war was over and peace had been declared. But they couldn't make those sailors believe it.

The sailors didn't dare to go into port, although they were out of water; but at last they made up their minds that it would be better to go in and surrender their cargo and surrender their lives to their enemies, than to perish at sea without water. But when they got in, they found out that peace had been declared after all, and that what had been told them was true.

Similarly, there are a great many people who don't believe the glad tidings that peace has already been made. Jesus Christ made peace on the cross. (See Colossians 1:20.) He satisfied the claims of the law; the law that condemns you and me has been fulfilled by Jesus Christ. He has made peace, and now He wants us just to enjoy it, just to believe it. There is not a thing to hinder us from doing this, if we will. We can enter into that blessing now and have perfect peace. The promise is:

> *Thou wilt keep him in perfect peace, whose mind is stayed on thee....Trust ye in the LORD for ever: for in the LORD JEHOVAH is everlasting strength.* (Isa. 26:3–4)

Now, as long as our minds are focused on ourselves, we will never have peace. Some people think more of themselves than of all the rest of the world. It is self in the morning, self at noon, and self at night. It is self when they wake up, and self when they go to bed; and they are all the time looking at themselves and thinking about themselves, instead of *"looking unto Jesus"* (Heb. 12:2). Faith looks outward. Faith does not look within; it looks out. It is not what I think, not what I feel, nor what I have done; it is what Jesus Christ is and has done.

Therefore, we should trust in Him who is our strength (Ps. 46:1) and whose strength will never fail. John told us that, after Christ rose from the grave, He met His disciples three times and said unto them, *"Peace be unto you"* (John 20:19,

21, 26). There is peace for the conscience through His blood and peace for the heart in His love. Remember, then, that love is power, and peace is power.

Secret of Joy

Now I will call attention to another fruit of the Spirit, and this, too, is power: the grace of joy. It is the privilege, I believe, of every Christian to walk in the light, as God is in the light (see 1 John 1:7) and to have that peace that flows unceasingly when we keep busy at His work. And it is our privilege to be full of the joy of the Lord. When Philip went down to Samaria and preached, there was great joy in the city. (See Acts 8:5–8.) Why? Because they believed the glad tidings. And that is the natural order: Joy comes after believing. When we believe the glad tidings, a joy comes into our souls.

We are told that our Lord sent the seventy out (see Luke 10:1), that they went forth preaching salvation in the name of Jesus Christ, and that a great many were blessed as a result of their preaching. The seventy returned, the Scripture says, *"with joy,"* and when they came back, they said that the very devils were subject to them, through His name (v. 17). The Lord seemed to correct them in this one thing when He said, *"Rejoice not, that the spirits are subject to you; but rather rejoice, because your names are written in heaven"* (v. 20). The seventy really had something to rejoice in now.

Let this be a word of assurance to you. God doesn't ask us to rejoice over nothing, but He gives us some ground for our joy. What would you think of a man who seemed very happy and full of joy, yet couldn't tell you what made him so? Suppose I were to meet a man on the street who was so full of joy that he got hold of both my hands and said, "Bless the Lord, I am so full of joy!"

"What makes you so full of joy?" I would ask.

"Well, I don't know."

"You don't know?"

"No, I don't; but I am so joyful that I just want to jump out of my flesh."

"What makes you feel so joyful?" I would inquire again.

"Well, I don't know."

Would we not think such a person unreasonable? But there are a great many people who feel—who want to feel—that they are Christians; they want the Christian's experience before they become Christians; they want to have the joy of the Lord before they receive Jesus Christ. But this is not the gospel order. He brings joy when He comes, and we cannot have joy apart from Him. There is no joy away from Him; He is the Author of it, and we find our joy in Him.

Perpetual Joy

Now, there are three kinds of joy. First, there is the joy of one's own salvation. I thought, when I first tasted this joy, that it was the most delightful joy I had ever known, and that I could never get beyond it. But I found, afterward, that there was something more joyful than that, namely, the joy of the salvation of others. Oh, the privilege, the blessed privilege, to be used by God to win a soul to Christ, to see a man or woman being led out of bondage by some act of ours toward them! To think that God condescends so far as to allow us to be coworkers with Him! It is the highest honor we can wear. This joy of seeing others saved surpasses even the joy of our own salvation.

John wrote that Jesus had no greater joy than to see His disciples walking in the truth. (See 3 John 1:4.) Every man who has been the means of leading souls to Christ understands what that means. So my advice to you, young disciples, is to walk in the truth, and you will have joy all the while.

But there is a third kind of joy, and we can find it in the difference between happiness and joy. Happiness is caused by things that happen around me. Oftentimes, circumstances will mar happiness, but joy flows right on through trouble. Joy flows on through the dark; joy flows in the night as well as in the day; joy flows all through persecution and opposition; it flows right along, for it is an unceasing fountain bubbling up in the heart, a secret spring that the world can't see and doesn't know anything about. The Lord gives His people perpetual joy when they walk in obedience to Him.

This joy is fed by the divine Word. Jeremiah said, in Jeremiah 15:16:

> *Thy words were found, and I did eat them; and thy word was unto me the joy and rejoicing of mine heart; for I am called by thy name, O LORD God of hosts.*

He ate the words, and what was the result? He said they were the joy and rejoicing of his heart. Now, people should look for joy in the Word, and not in the world. They should look for the joy that the Scriptures furnish and then go work in the vineyard, because a joy that doesn't send me out to someone else, a joy that doesn't impel me to go and help the poor drunkard, a joy that doesn't prompt me to visit the widow and the fatherless, a joy that doesn't cause me to help with the Sunday school or to do other Christian work, is not worth having and is not from above. A joy that does not cause me to go and work for the Master is purely sentiment and not real joy.

Joy in Persecution

> *Blessed are ye, when men shall hate you, and when they shall separate you from their*

*company, and shall reproach you, and cast out
your name as evil, for the Son of man's sake.
Rejoice ye in that day, and leap for joy: for,
behold, your reward is great in heaven: for
in the like manner did their fathers unto the
prophets.* (Luke 6:22–23)

As Christians, we do not receive our reward on
this earth. We have to go against the current of the
world. We may be unpopular, and we may have to
go against many of our personal friends, because
we live godly lives in Christ Jesus. Yet, at the same
time, if we are persecuted for the Master's sake,
we will have this joy bubbling up; it will just come
right up into our hearts all the while—a joy that
is unceasing, a joy that flows right on. The world
cannot choke that fountain. If we have Christ in
our hearts, the reward will come soon enough.

The longer I live, the more I am convinced that
godly men and women are not appreciated in our
day. But their work will live after them, and there
will be a greater work done after they are gone, by
the influence of their lives, than when they were
living. Daniel is doing a thousand times more today
than when he was living in Babylon. Abraham is
doing more today than he did on the plain with his
tent and altar. He has been living all these centuries, and so we read:

*Blessed are the dead which die in the Lord
from henceforth: Yea, saith the Spirit, that they*

may rest from their labours; and their works do follow them. (Rev. 14:13)

Let us set the streams running that will flow on after we have gone. If we have persecution and opposition today, let us press forward, and our reward will be great before long. Oh, think of this! The Lord Jesus, the Maker of heaven and earth, who created the world, says, *"Your reward shall be great"* (Luke 6:35). He calls it great. If some friend should say it is great, it might be very small; but when the Lord, the great and mighty God, says it is great, what must it be? Oh, the reward that is in store for those who serve Him! We have this joy, if we serve Him.

A man who is cast down is not fit to work for God, because he goes about his work with a telltale face. *"The joy of the LORD is your strength"* (Neh. 8:10). What we need today is a joyful church. A joyful church will make inroads upon the works of Satan, and we will see the Gospel going down into dark lanes and dark alleys, and into dark garrets and cellars. We will see the drunkards reached, and the gamblers and the harlots will come pressing into the kingdom of God.

It is this carrying a sad countenance, with so many wrinkles on our brows, that delays the progress of Christianity. Oh, may great joy come upon believers everywhere, that we may shout for joy and rejoice in God day and night! A joyful church—let us pray for that, that the Lord may make us joyful;

and when we have joy, then we will have success. And if we don't have the reward we think we should have here, let us constantly remember the rewarding time that is to come.

Someone has said, if you had asked men in Abraham's day who their great man was, they would have said Enoch, not Abraham. If you had asked in Moses's day who their great man was, they would not have said it was Moses, for he was nothing; it would have been Abraham. If you had asked in the days of Elijah or Daniel, it wouldn't have been Daniel or Elijah, for they were nothing; it would have been Moses. And in the days of Jesus Christ, if you had asked about John the Baptist or the apostles, you would have heard that these men were lowly and contemptible in the sight of the world and were looked upon with scorn and reproach. But see how mighty they have become.

And so, we will not be appreciated in our day, but we are to toil on and work on, possessing this fountain of joy all the while. And if we lack it, let us cry:

Restore unto me the joy of thy salvation; and uphold me with thy free spirit. Then will I teach transgressors thy ways; and sinners shall be converted unto thee. (Ps. 51:12–13)

Again, John 15:11 reads, *"These things have I spoken unto you, that my joy might remain in you, and that your joy might be full."* And in the sixteenth chapter, we find:

> *And ye now therefore have sorrow: but I will see you again, and your heart shall rejoice, and your joy no man taketh from you.*
>
> (John 16:22)

I am so thankful that I have a joy that the world cannot rob me of; I have a treasure that the world cannot take from me; I have something that is not in the power of man or devil to deprive me of, and that is the joy of the Lord. *"No man taketh* [it] *from you."*

In the second century, a martyr was brought before a king, and the king demanded him to recant and give up Christ and Christianity. But the man spurned the proposition. The king said, "If you don't do it, I will banish you."

The man smiled and answered, "You can't banish me from Christ, for He says He will never leave me nor forsake me." (See Hebrews 13:5.)

The king became angry. "Well," he said, "I will confiscate your property and take it all from you."

And the man replied, "My treasures are laid up on high; you cannot get them." (See Matthew 6:20.)

The king became still angrier, saying, "I will kill you."

"Why," the man answered, "I have been dead forty years; I have been dead with Christ, dead to the world, and my life is hidden with Christ in God. You cannot touch it." (See Colossians 3:3.)

And so, we can rejoice, because we are on resurrection ground, having risen with Christ. (See Colossians 3:1.) Let persecution and opposition come; we can rejoice continually. And let us remember that our reward is great, reserved for us (see 1 Peter 1:3–4) unto the Day when He who is our Life shall appear, and we shall appear with Him in glory (Col. 3:4).

Chapter Three

Power Hindered

Chapter Three

Power Hindered

T hus far I have written of the power available to us through the Holy Spirit of God. We have seen that this power is manifested in our lives through the fruits of the Spirit, especially love, peace, and joy. But so many professing Christians do not have this power of the Holy Spirit. What is hindering them from producing the fruits of the Spirit and from living in power? This is what we must come to understand.

The Unpardonable Sin

We are told in the Scriptures that Israel limited God. They vexed and grieved the Holy Spirit and rebelled against His authority. But there is a special sin against the Spirit that we must consider, and it will benefit us to understand it. The first description of it begins in Matthew 12:22:

Then was brought unto him one possessed with a devil, blind, and dumb: and he healed him, insomuch that the blind and dumb both spake and saw. And all the people were amazed, and said, Is not this the son of David? But when the Pharisees heard it, they said, This fellow doth not cast out devils, but by Beelzebub the prince of the devils. And Jesus knew their thoughts, and said unto them, Every kingdom divided against itself is brought to desolation; and every city or house divided against itself shall not stand: and if Satan cast out Satan, he is divided against himself; how shall then his kingdom stand? And if I by Beelzebub cast out devils, by whom do your children cast them out? therefore they shall be your judges. But if I cast out devils by the Spirit of God, then the kingdom of God is come unto you. Or else how can one enter into a strong man's house, and spoil his goods, except he first bind the strong man? and then he will spoil his house. He that is not with me is against me; and he that gathereth not with me scattereth abroad. Wherefore I say unto you, All manner of sin and blasphemy shall be forgiven unto men: but the blasphemy against the Holy Ghost shall not be forgiven unto men. And whosoever speaketh a word against the Son of man, it shall be forgiven him: but whosoever speaketh against the Holy Ghost, it shall not be forgiven him, neither in this world, neither in the world to come. (Matt. 12:22–32)

That is Matthew's account. Now read Mark's account.

> *And when his friends heard of it, they went out to lay hold on him: for they said, He [that is, Christ] is beside himself. And the scribes which came down from Jerusalem said, He hath Beelzebub, and by the prince of devils casteth he out devils.* (Mark 3:21–22)

The word *Beelzebub* means "the Lord of Filth." They charged the Lord Jesus with being possessed not only with an evil spirit, but also with having a filthy spirit.

> *And he called them unto him, and said unto them in parables, How can Satan cast out Satan? And if a kingdom be divided against itself, that kingdom cannot stand. And if a house be divided against itself, that house cannot stand. And if Satan rise up against himself, and be divided, he cannot stand, but hath an end. No man can enter into a strong man's house, and spoil his goods, except he will first bind the strong man; and then he will spoil his house. Verily I say unto you, All sins shall be forgiven unto the sons of men, and blasphemies wherewith soever they shall blaspheme: but he that shall blaspheme against the Holy Ghost hath never forgiveness, but is in danger of eternal damnation.* (Mark 3:23–29)

Now, if it stopped there, we would, perhaps, be left in darkness, and we would not exactly understand what the sin against the Holy Spirit is. But, the next verse of this same chapter of Mark throws light upon the whole matter, and we need not be in darkness another minute if we really want light, for, observe, the verse reads, *"Because they said, He hath an unclean spirit"* (v. 30).

I don't believe any man has any right to say he has committed the unpardonable sin—the sin of blaspheming the Holy Spirit—unless he has maliciously and willfully and deliberately said that he believes Jesus Christ had a devil in Him, that He was under the power of the Devil, and that He cast out devils by the power of the Devil. Now, I have met a good many atheists and skeptics and deists and infidels, both in this country and abroad, but I never in my life met a man or woman who ever said that Jesus Christ was possessed by an unclean devil. Have you? I don't think you ever met such a person. I have heard men say bitter things against Christ, but I never heard any man stand up and say that he thought Jesus Christ was possessed with the Devil.

Yet, perhaps you have heard someone say that there is such a thing as grieving the Spirit of God and resisting the Spirit of God, until He has taken His flight and left you. Perhaps you have said, "That is the unpardonable sin." However, there is a misunderstanding here. We need to take the Scripture passages and clarify what it means to resist the Spirit, what it means to grieve the Spirit, and what it means to commit the unpardonable sin. For to resist or to grieve the Holy Spirit is one thing, but to commit that awful sin of blasphemy against the Holy Spirit is quite another.

What It Is Not

I admit there is such a thing as resisting the Spirit of God, and even resisting until the Spirit of God has departed; but if the Spirit of God has left anyone, that person will not be troubled about his sins. The very fact that he is troubled shows that the Spirit of God has not left him. If a man is troubled about his sins, it is the work of the Spirit, not the work of Satan.

Satan makes us believe that we are pretty good, that we are good enough without God, safe without Christ, and that we don't need salvation. But when a man wakes up to the fact that he is lost, that he is a sinner, it is the work of the Spirit; and if the Spirit of God had left him, he would not be in that state. When men and women want to be Christians, it is a sign that the Spirit of God is drawing them.

If resisting the Spirit of God is an unpardonable sin, then we have all committed it, and there is no hope for any of us; for I do not believe there is a minister, or a worker in Christ's vineyard, who has not, at some time in his life, resisted or rejected the Spirit of God. Stephen charged the unbelieving Jews, *"Ye do always resist the Holy Ghost: as your fathers did, so do ye"* (Acts 7:51). The world has always been resisting the Spirit of God. That is the history of the world in every age. In keeping with this, the world today is resisting the Holy Spirit.

"Faithful are the wounds of a friend" (Prov. 27:6). The divine Spirit, as a friend, reveals to this poor world its faults, and the world only hates Him for it. He shows them the plague of their hearts. He convinces or convicts them of sin (see John 16:8); therefore, they fight the Spirit of God. I believe there is many a man today fighting against and resisting the Holy Spirit of God.

Bad Thoughts

Some people say, "I have such blasphemous thoughts; there are some awful thoughts that come into my mind against God," and they think that is the unpardonable sin. But we are not to blame for having bad thoughts come into our minds. If we harbor them, however, then we are to blame. But if the Devil comes and darts an evil thought into my mind, and I say, "Lord, help me," sin is not reckoned to me. Who has not had evil thoughts come into his mind or flash into his heart and not been called to fight them?

One theologian has said, "You are not to blame for the birds that fly over your head, but if you allow them to come down and make a nest in your hair, then you are to blame. You are to blame if you don't fight them off." And so it is with these evil thoughts that come flashing into our minds. We have to fight them; we are not to harbor them; we are not to entertain them. If I have evil thoughts and evil desires come into my mind, it is no sign that I have committed the unpardonable sin. However, if I love these thoughts and harbor them, and think evil of God, and think Jesus Christ a blasphemer, then I am responsible for gross iniquity. If I charge Him with being the prince of devils, then I am committing the unpardonable sin.

Grieving the Spirit

Let us now consider the sin of grieving the Spirit. Resisting the Holy Spirit is one thing, but grieving Him is another. In Ephesians 4:30–32 we read:

> *And grieve not the holy Spirit of God, whereby ye are sealed unto the day of redemption. Let all bitterness, and wrath, and anger, and clamour, and evil speaking, be put away from you, with all malice: and be ye kind one to another, tenderhearted, forgiving one another, even as God for Christ's sake hath forgiven you.*

Now, notice that these words were written to the church at Ephesus. *"Grieve not the holy Spirit of God, whereby ye are sealed unto the day of redemption."* I believe that the church all over Christendom today is guilty of grieving the Holy Spirit. Look around.

You will see there are a good many believers in different churches wondering why the work of God is not revived.

What the Church Is Doing

I think that if we search enough, we will find something in the church grieving the Spirit of God. It may be a mere schism in the church; it may be some unsound doctrine; it may be some division in the church. Yet there is one thing I have noticed as I have traveled in different countries: I never yet have known the Spirit of God to work where the Lord's people were divided. As a result, there is one thing that we must have if we are to have the Holy Spirit of God working in our midst, and that is unity.

If a church is divided, the members should immediately seek unity. Let the believers come together and get the difficulty out of the way. If the minister of a church cannot unite the people, if those who are dissatisfied will not fall in with the rest, then it would be better for that minister to retire. I think there are a good many ministers in this country who are wasting their time. Some of them have lost months, and some of them, years. They have not seen any fruit, and they will not see any fruit, because they have a divided church. Such a church cannot grow in divine things. The Spirit of God doesn't work where there is division, and what we need today is the spirit of unity among God's children, so that the Lord may work.

Worldly Amusements

Another thing that grieves the Spirit, I think, is the miserable policy of introducing questionable entertainments into the church. There are the lotteries, for instance, that we have in many churches. If a man wants to gamble, he doesn't have to go to some gambling den; he can stay right in the church. And there are fairs—bazaars, as they call them—where they have raffles and grab bags. And if a man wants to see a drama, he doesn't need to go to the theater, for many of our churches are sometimes turned into theaters; he may stay right in the church and see the performance. I believe all these things grieve the Spirit of God. I believe that when we bring the church down to the level of the world, although we are doing so in order to reach the world, we are losing and grieving the Spirit of God all the while.

But, some say, if we take that standard and lift it up high, it will drive away a great many members from our churches. This I believe, and I think the quicker they are gone the better. The world has come into the church like a flood, and how often you find an ungodly choir employed to do the singing for the whole congregation. The idea that we need an ungodly man to sing praises to God!

Unconverted Choirs

It was not long ago that I heard of a church where they had an unconverted choir. The minister saw something about the choir that he didn't like, and he spoke to the choir director about it, but the choir director replied, "You attend to your end of the church, and I will attend to mine." You cannot expect the Spirit of God to work in a church in such a state as that.

Paul told us not to speak in an unknown tongue (see 1 Corinthians 14:2–5), and if we have choirs who are singing in an unknown tongue, why isn't that just as great an abomination? I have been in churches where they have had a choir who would rise and sing and sing, and it seemed as if they sang for five or ten minutes, but I could not understand one solitary word they sang. And all the while, the people were looking around carelessly.

There are, perhaps, a select few who are very fond of fine music, and they want to bring the opera right into the church. So they have opera music in the church, and the people, who are drowsy and sleepy, don't take part in the singing. The ungodly, unconverted men who are hired to present the music will sit back in the choir loft and, the moment the minister begins his sermon, will take out their Sunday papers and read them the whole time the minister is preaching. The organist, provided he does not go out for a walk, will read his paper, or perhaps a novel, if he happens to keep awake while the minister is preaching.

Meanwhile, the minister wonders why God doesn't revive His work in the church; he wonders why he is losing his hold on the congregation; he wonders why people don't come crowding into the church, why people are running after the world instead. The trouble is that we have let down the standard; we have grieved the Spirit of God. One movement of God's power is worth more than all our artificial power, and what the church of God needs today is to get down in the dust of humiliation and confession of sin and to be separated from the world. Then we may see if we do not have power with God and with men.

What Is Success?

The Gospel has not lost its power; it is just as powerful today as it ever has been. We don't need any new doctrine. It is still the old Gospel with the old power, the Holy Spirit power; and if the churches will confess their sins and put them away, lifting the standard instead of pulling it down and praying to God to lift us up into the higher and holier life, then the fear of the Lord will come upon the people around us.

It was when Jacob put away strange gods and set his face toward Bethel that the fear of God fell upon the surrounding nations. (See Genesis 35:2–5.) And when the churches turn toward God, when we cease grieving the Spirit so that He may work through us, then we will have conversions all the time. Believers will be added to the church daily.

It is sad when you look over Christendom and see how desolate it is, how little spiritual life and spiritual power there is in the church of God today. Many of the church members do not even desire this Holy Spirit power. They don't desire it; they want intellectual power. They want to get some man who will just draw the people into the church. They want a choir that will draw. They do not care whether anyone is saved; with them, that is not the question. They want only to fill the pews, have good society, fashionable people, and dancing.

Such people are found one night at the theater and the next night at the opera. They don't like the prayer meetings—they abhor them; and if the minister would only lecture and entertain, that would please them.

I said to a man some time ago, "How are you getting on at your church?"

"Oh, splendid," was his reply.

"Many conversions?"

"Well—well, on that side we are not getting on so well. But," he said, "we rented all our pews and are able to pay all our running expenses; we are getting on splendidly."

That is what the godless call "getting on splendidly"—because they rent the pews, pay the minister, and pay all the running expenses. Conversions! That is a strange word to their ears.

Power Hindered

There was a man being shown through one of the cathedrals of Europe. He had come in from the country, and one of the men belonging to the cathedral was showing him around. The visitor inquired, "Do you have many conversions here?"

"Many what?"

"Many conversions here?"

"Ah, man, this is not a Wesleyan chapel." To him, the idea of there being conversions there was absurd, almost meaningless! And you can go into a good many churches in this country and ask if they have many conversions, and they would not know what you meant—they are so far away from the Lord. They are not looking for conversions, nor do they expect them.

Shipwrecks

Alas! How many young converts have been shipwrecked against such churches! Instead of being a harbor of delight to them, these churches have proved to be false lights, luring them to destruction. Isn't it time for us to get down on our faces before God and cry mightily to Him to forgive our sins? The quicker we admit them, the better.

Suppose you are invited to a party, and the attendees are all church members. What will the conversation be about? I got so sick and tired of such parties that I left them behind years ago. I would not think of spending a night that way again;

it is a waste of time; there is hardly a chance to say a word for the Master. If you talk about a personal Christ, your presence becomes offensive; they don't like it. They want you to talk about the world, about a popular minister, a popular church, a good organ, or a good choir. They will say, "Oh, we have a grand organ, and a superb choir," and all that, and it suits them fine; but that doesn't warm the Christian heart. When you speak of a risen Christ and a personal Savior, they don't like it. The fact is, the world has come into the church and taken possession of it, and what we need to do is wake up and ask God to forgive us for grieving His Spirit.

Dear reader, search your heart and inquire, "Have I done anything to grieve the Spirit of God?" If you have, may God show it to you today. If you have done anything to grieve the Spirit of God, you need to find it out today and get down on your face before God and ask Him to forgive you and help you put it away. I have lived long enough to know that if I cannot have the power of the Spirit of God on me to help me work for Him, I would rather die than live just for the sake of living. How many are there in the church today who have been members for fifteen or twenty years, but have never done a single thing for Jesus Christ? They cannot identify one solitary soul who has been blessed through their influence; they cannot point to even one person who has ever been lifted up by them.

Power Hindered

Quench Not

In 1 Thessalonians 5:19 we are told, *"Quench not the Spirit."* Now, I am confident that, for a great many, the cares of the world are coming in and quenching the Spirit. Many people say, "I don't care for the world." Perhaps they don't care for the pleasures of the world so much, after all, but they have let the cares of this life come into their lives and quench the Spirit of God.

Anything that comes between me and God— between my soul and God—quenches the Spirit. It may be my family. You may say, "How can there be any danger of loving my family too much?" Well, there is no danger if you love God more. God must have the first place. If I love my family more than I love God, then I am quenching the Spirit of God within me. If I love wealth, if I love fame, if I love honor, if I love position, if I love pleasure, if I love self more than I love God, who created and saved me, then I am committing a sin. I am not only grieving the Spirit of God but quenching Him and robbing my soul of His power.

Oh, that we may know Him in all His wealth of blessing! This is my prayer for myself, as well as for you. And may we heed the words of the apostle Paul:

My speech and my preaching was not with enticing words of man's wisdom, but in

*demonstration of the Spirit and of power: that
your faith should not stand in the wisdom of
men, but in the power of God.*

(1 Cor. 2:4–5)

Chapter Four

Power "In" and "Upon"

Chapter Four

Power "In" and "Upon"

The Holy Spirit dwelling in us is one thing, and the Holy Spirit upon us for service is another thing. I think this is clearly brought out in Scripture. Beginning in Exodus 40:33, we read the following words:

> And he [that is, Moses] *reared up the court round about the tabernacle and the altar, and set up the hanging of the court gate. So Moses finished the work. Then a cloud covered the tent of the congregation, and the glory of the* LORD *filled the tabernacle. And Moses was not able to enter into the tent of the congregation, because the cloud abode thereon, and the glory of the* LORD *filled the tabernacle.* (Exod. 40:33–35)

The moment that Moses finished the work, the moment that the tabernacle was ready, the cloud came, the Shekinah glory came and filled it so that Moses was not able to stand before the presence of the Lord.

Our Hearts, His Dwelling Place

I firmly believe that the moment our hearts are emptied of selfishness and ambition and self-seeking and everything that is contrary to God's law, the Holy Spirit will come and fill every corner of our hearts; but if we are full of pride and conceit, ambition and self-seeking, pleasure and the world, there is no room for the Spirit of God. I also believe that many a man is praying to God to fill him, when he is full already with something else. Before we pray that God would fill us, I believe we ought to pray that He would empty us.

There must be an emptying before there can be a filling; and when the heart is turned upside down, and everything that is contrary to God is turned out, then the Spirit will come, just as He did in the tabernacle, and fill us with His glory. We read in 2 Chronicles 5:13–14:

> *It came even to pass, as the trumpeters and singers were as one, to make one sound to be heard in praising and thanking the LORD; and when they lifted up their voice with the trumpets and cymbals and instruments of music, and praised the LORD, saying, For he is good; for his mercy endureth for ever: that then the house was filled with a cloud, even the house of*

the LORD; so that the priests could not stand to minister by reason of the cloud: for the glory of the LORD had filled the house of God.

We find in the Scriptures that, at the very moment Solomon completed the temple and all was finished, the people were praising God with one heart. The choristers and the singers and the ministers were all one; there was not any discord. They were all praising God, and the glory of God came and just filled the temple as a dwelling place. Now, as you turn over into the New Testament, you will find that believers, instead of tabernacles and temples, are now the dwelling place of the Holy Spirit. (See John 14:17.)

On the Day of Pentecost, before Peter preached that memorable sermon, the Holy Spirit came as they were praying, and He came in mighty power. We pray now for the Spirit of God to come, and we sing:

> Come, Holy Spirit, heavenly dove,
>   With all thy quickening power;
> Kindle a flame of heavenly love
>   In these cold hearts of ours.

I believe that it is perfectly right for us to pray in this way, if we understand it; but if we are praying for Him to come out of heaven and down to earth again, that is wrong, because He is already here. The Holy Spirit has not been absent from this earth for nineteen hundred years; He has been in the church, and He is with all believers. The believers in the church are the called-out ones; they are called out from the world, and every true believer is a temple for the Holy Spirit to dwell in.

In John 14:17 we have the words of Jesus:

The Spirit of truth; whom the world cannot receive, because it seeth him not, neither knoweth him: but ye know him; for he dwelleth with you, and shall be in you.

"Greater is he that is in you, than he that is in the world" (1 John 4:4). If we have the Spirit dwelling in us, He gives us power over the flesh and the world, and over every enemy. *"He dwelleth with you, and shall be in you."*

Read 1 Corinthians 3:16: *"Know ye not that ye are the temple of God, and that the Spirit of God dwelleth in you?"*

There were some men burying an aged saint some time ago. He was very poor, like many of God's people: They are poor in this world, but they are very rich; they have all the riches on the other side of life; they have laid up their riches where thieves cannot get them, where swindlers cannot take them away from them, and where moths cannot corrupt them. (See Matthew 6:19–20.) This aged man, likewise, was very rich in the other world, and they were just hastening him off to the grave, wanting to get rid of him, when an old minister, who was officiating at the grave, said, "Tread softly, for you are carrying the temple of the Holy Ghost." Whenever you see a believer, you see a temple of the Holy Spirit.

In 1 Corinthians 6:19–20, we read again:

Know ye not that your body is the temple of the Holy Ghost which is in you, which ye have of God, and ye are not your own? For ye are bought with a price: therefore glorify God in your body, and in your spirit, which are God's.

Thus are we taught that there is a divine resident in every child of God.

I think it is clearly taught in the Scriptures that every believer has the Holy Spirit dwelling in him. He may be quenching the Spirit of God, and he may not glorify God as he should, but if he is a believer in the Lord Jesus Christ, the Holy Spirit dwells in him. I want to call your attention to another fact.

What Is Needed

I believe that, although Christian men and women have the Holy Spirit dwelling in them, He is not dwelling within them in power. In other words, God has a great many sons and daughters without power. At least nine-tenths of church members never think of speaking for Christ. If they see a man, perhaps a near relative, going rapidly down to ruin, they never think of speaking to him about his sinful course and of seeking to win him to Christ.

Now, certainly, there must be something wrong. And yet, when you talk with them, you find they have faith, and you cannot say they are not children of God. But they do not have the power, they do not have the liberty, they do not have the love, that real disciples of Christ should have.

A great many people are thinking that we need new methods, that we need new churches, that we need new organs, that we need new choirs, and all these new things. That is not what the church of God needs today. Rather, we need the old power that the apostles had; that is what we lack, and if we have that in our churches, there will be new life. Then we will have new ministers—the same old ministers renewed with power and filled with the Spirit.

I remember when I was in Chicago, and many were toiling in the work of the Gospel, and it seemed as though the chariot of salvation didn't move on. A minister there began to cry out from the very depths of his heart, "O God, put new ministers in every pulpit." And on the following Monday, two or three men stood up and said, "We had a new minister last Sunday—the same old minister, but he had new power."

I firmly believe that this is what we need today all over America. We need new ministers in the pulpit and new people in the pews. We need people who are quickened by the Spirit of God, and we need the Spirit to come down and take possession of the children of God and give them power. Then a man filled with the Spirit will know how to use *"the sword of the Spirit"* (Eph. 6:17).

If a man is not filled with the Spirit, he will never know how to use the Book. We are told that this is the sword of the Spirit; and what good is an army that does not know how to use its weapons? Suppose a battle were going on, and I was a general with a hundred thousand men—great, able-bodied men, full of life—but not one of them could handle a sword, and not one of them knew how to use his rifle. What would that army be good for? Why, one thousand well-drilled men with good weapons would rout the whole lot of them.

The reason the church cannot overcome the Enemy is because she doesn't know how to use the sword of the Spirit. People will get up and try to fight the Devil with their experiences, but he doesn't care for that; he will overcome them every time. People are trying to fight the Devil with theories and pet ideas, but he will get the victory over them likewise. What we need is to draw the sword of the Spirit. It is that which cuts deeper than anything else.

Turn in your Bible to Ephesians 6:14–17, and you will read:

Stand therefore, having your loins girt about with truth, and having on the breastplate of righteousness; and your feet shod with the preparation of the gospel of peace; above all, taking the shield of faith, wherewith ye shall be able to quench all the fiery darts of the wicked. And take the helmet of salvation, and the sword of the Spirit, which is the word of God.

The Greatest Weapon

The sword of the Spirit is the Word of God, and what we need especially is to be filled with the Spirit so that we will know how to use the Word. A Christian man, while talking to a skeptic, was using the Word, and the skeptic said, "Sir, I don't believe in that Book." But the man went right on witnessing and gave him more of the Word, and the skeptic again remarked, "I don't believe the Word." But he kept giving him more, and at last the man was reached. And the brother added, "When I have proved a good sword that does the work of execution, I will just keep right on using it."

That is what we need. Skeptics and infidels may say they don't believe in it, but it is not our work to make them believe in it; that is the work of the Spirit. Our work is to give them the Word of God, not to preach our theories and our ideas about it, but just to deliver the message as God gives it to us.

We read in the Scriptures of the sword of the Lord and Gideon. (See Judges 7:15–22.) Suppose that Gideon had gone out without the Word; he would have been defeated. But the Lord used Gideon, and I think you find all through the Scriptures that God takes up and uses human instruments. You cannot find, I believe, a case in the Bible where a man is converted without God calling in some human agency, using some human instrument. Certainly, in His independent sovereignty, He can do it without the human instrument; there is no doubt about that. But that is not His way; that is not His method. Even when, by the revealed glory of the Lord Jesus, Saul of Tarsus was smitten to the earth, Ananias was used to open his eyes and lead him into the light of the Gospel.

I heard a man once say that if you put a man on a mountain peak, higher than one of the Alpine peaks, God could save him without a human messenger. But Scripture speaks of *"the sword of the Lord, and of Gideon"* (Judges 7:18), and the Lord and Gideon will do the work. If we are simply willing to let the Lord use us, He will.

None of Self

You will find that, all through the Scriptures, when men were filled with the Holy Spirit, they preached Christ and not themselves. They preached Christ and Him crucified. (See 1 Corinthians 2:2.) In the first chapter of Luke, the Scriptures tell of Zacharias, the father of John the Baptist:

And his father Zacharias was filled with the Holy Ghost, and prophesied, saying, Blessed be the Lord God of Israel; for he hath visited and redeemed his people, and hath raised up an horn of salvation for us in the house of his servant David; as he spake by the mouth of his holy prophets, which have been since the world began. (Luke 1:67–70)

These verses are all about the Word. If a man is filled with the Spirit, he will magnify the Word; he will preach the Word, and not himself; he will give this lost world the Word of the living God.

And thou, child, shalt be called the prophet of the Highest: for thou shalt go before the face of the Lord to prepare his ways; to give knowledge of salvation unto his people by the remission of their sins, through the tender mercy of our God; whereby the dayspring from on high hath visited us, to give light to them that sit in darkness and in the shadow of death, to guide our feet into the way of peace. And the child grew, and waxed strong in spirit, and was in the deserts till the day of his showing unto Israel. (Luke 1:76–80)

And so we find that when Elizabeth and Mary met, they talked of the Scriptures, and they were both filled with the Holy Spirit and at once began to talk of their Lord.

We also find that Simeon, as he came into the temple and found the young child Jesus there, at once began to quote the Scriptures, for the Spirit was upon him. (See Luke 2:27–35.) And when Peter stood up on the Day of Pentecost and preached that wonderful sermon, it is said he was filled with the Holy Spirit and began to preach the Word to the multitude, and it was the Word that cut them. (See Acts 2:1–37.) It was the sword of the Lord and Peter, just as it was the sword of the Lord and Gideon.

The Scriptures say of Stephen, *"They were not able to resist the wisdom and the spirit by which he spake"* (Acts 6:10). Why? Because he gave them the Word of God. And we are told that the Holy Spirit came on Stephen and that none could resist his words. And we read, too, that Paul was full of the Holy Spirit, that he preached Christ and Him crucified, and that many people were added to the church. Barnabas was full of faith and the Holy Spirit, and, if you read the Scriptures, you will find that what he preached was the Word and that many were added to the Lord. So, when a man is full of the Spirit, he begins to preach, not himself, but Christ, as revealed in the Holy Scriptures.

The disciples of Jesus were all filled with the Spirit, and the Word was published; when the Spirit of God comes down upon the church and we are anointed, the Word will be published in the streets, in the lanes, and in the alleys. If the Spirit comes upon God's people in demonstration and in power, there will not be a dark cellar, a dark attic, or a dark home into which the Gospel will not be carried by some loving heart.

Spiritual Irrigation

It is possible that a man may just barely have life and be satisfied, and I think that a great many people are in that condition. In John 3 we find that Nicodemus came to Christ and that he received life. At first this life was feeble. You don't hear of him standing up and confessing Christ boldly or of the Spirit coming upon him in great power, although he possessed life through faith in Christ.

The woman who came to the well of Samaria, in John 4, took the cup of salvation that Christ held out to her, and she drank, and it became in her *"a well of water springing up into everlasting life"* (John 4:14). That is better than what Nicodemus experienced; here it came down in a flood into her soul. Someone has said that it came down from the throne of God and, like a mighty current, carried her back to the throne of God. Water always rises to its level, and if we get the soul filled with water from the throne of God, it will bear us upward to its Source.

But the best kind of Christian life is portrayed in the seventh chapter of John. You will find that it says of anyone who receives the Spirit through trusting in the Lord Jesus, *"out of his belly shall flow rivers of living water"* (John 7:38).

Now, there are two ways of digging a well. When I was a boy, I lived on a farm in New England. I remember there was a well with an old wooden pump, and I used to have to pump the water from that well in order to have water for the laundry and for the cattle. I had to pump and pump and pump until my arm got tired, many a time.

But there is a better way now. When a well is dug, the men don't dig down a few feet and brick up the hole and put the pump in. No, they go down through the clay and the sand and the rock and on down until they strike what they call a lower stream, and then it becomes an artesian well, which needs no labor because the water rises spontaneously from the depths below.

Now, I think God wants all His children to be a sort of artesian well: not to keep pumping, but to flow right out. Haven't you seen ministers in the pulpit just pumping and pumping and pumping? I have, many a time, and I have had to do it, too. I know how it is. They stand at the pulpit and talk and talk and talk, and the people go to sleep; they can't wake them. What is the trouble? The living water is not there; they are just pumping, when there is no water in the well! You can't get water out of a dry well; you need to have something in the well, or you can't get anything out.

I have seen wooden pumps into which you had to pour water before you could pump any water out. It is the same with a good many people; you have to put something in them before you can get anything out. People wonder why it is that they have no spiritual power. They stand up and talk in prayer meetings, but they don't say anything. They will tell you that they haven't anything to say, and you find it out soon enough; they do not need to state it. Nevertheless, they just talk because they feel it is a duty, yet they say nothing.

Now, when the Spirit of God is on us for service, resting upon us, we are anointed, and then we can do great things. *"I will pour water upon him that is thirsty"* (Isa. 44:3), says God. Oh, blessed thought! He that hungers and thirsts after righteousness shall be filled! (See Matthew 5:6.)

Outflowing Streams

I would like to see someone who is full of living water—so full that he cannot contain it, so full that he has to go out and publish the Gospel of the grace of God. When a man gets so full that he can't hold any more, then he is ready for God's service.

When he was preaching in Chicago, Dr. Gibson put forth the question, How can we find out who is thirsty? And he said, "I was just thinking how we could find out. If a boy were to come down the aisle, bringing a bucket full of clear water and a dipper, we would soon find out who was thirsty; we would see thirsty men and women reach out for water. But if he were to walk down the aisle with an empty bucket, we wouldn't find it out. People would look in and see that there was no water and say nothing. I think that is the reason we are not more blessed in our ministry; we are carrying around empty buckets, the people see that we do not have anything in them, and they don't come forward."

I think that there is a good deal of truth in what he said. People see that we are carrying around empty buckets, and they will not come to us until they are filled. They see we haven't any more of God's power than they have. We must have the Spirit of God resting upon us, and then we will have something that gives victory over the world, the flesh, and the Devil; something that gives victory over our tempers, our conceits, and every other evil. When we can trample these sins under our feet, then people will come to us and say, "How did you get this power? You have something that I do not have, and I need it." Oh, may God show us this truth!

Have we been toiling all night? Let us throw the net on the right side (see John 21:5–6); let us ask God to forgive our sins and anoint us with power from on high. But remember, He is not going to give this power to an impatient man; He is not going to give it to a selfish man; He will never give it to an ambitious man whose aim is selfish, until he is first emptied of self, emptied of pride, and emptied of all worldly thoughts. Let it be God's glory and not our own that we seek, and when we get to that point, how speedily the Lord will bless us for good! Then will the measure of our blessing be full.

Do you know what heaven's measure is? *"Good measure, pressed down, and shaken together, and running over"* (Luke 6:38). If we get our hearts filled with the Spirit and the Word of God, how is Satan going to get in? He is not going to get in, and the world is not going to get in, for heaven's measure is good measure, full measure, running over.

Do you have this fullness? If you don't, then seek it. Say it aloud that, by the grace of God, you will have it, for it is the Father's good pleasure to give us these things. (See Luke 12:32.) He wants us to shine down in this world; He wants to lift us up for His work; He wants us to have the power to testify for His Son. He has placed us in this world to testify for Him, not to buy and sell and make a profit, but to glorify Christ. How are you going to do it without the Spirit? That is the question. How are you going to do it without the power of God?

Why Some Fail

We read in John 20:22, *"And when he had said this, he breathed on them, and saith unto them, Receive ye the Holy Ghost."* Then we see in Luke 24:49:

And, behold. I send the promise of my Father upon you: but tarry ye in the city of Jerusalem, until ye be endued with power from on high.

The first passage tells us that Christ had raised those pierced and wounded hands over the disciples and breathed upon them and said, *"Receive ye the Holy Ghost."* I do not doubt that they received it then, but the Spirit had yet to come in mighty power, to qualify them for their work. He did not give the Holy Spirit to them in fullness then, but if they had been like a good many people today, each of them would have said, "I have enough now; I am not going to tarry; I am going to work."

Some people seem to think they are losing time if they wait on God for His power, and so they go and work without any anointing; they are working without any power. But after Jesus had said, *"Receive ye the Holy Ghost,"* and had breathed on the disciples, He said, *"But tarry ye in the city of Jerusalem, until ye be endued with power from on high."* Acts 1:8 says, *"But ye shall receive power,* [when] *the Holy Ghost is come upon you."*

Now, the Spirit had certainly been given to them, or they could not have believed, and they could not have taken their stand for God and gone through what they did. They could not have endured the scoffs and frowns of their friends, if they had not been converted by the power of the Holy Spirit. But now, just see what Christ said:

> *Ye shall receive power,* [when] *the Holy Ghost is come upon you: and ye shall be witnesses unto me both in Jerusalem, and in all Judaea, and*

in Samaria, and unto the uttermost part of the earth. (Acts 1:8)

The Holy Spirit *in us* is one thing, and the Holy Spirit *upon us* is another. If these Christians had gone right to preaching then and there, without the power, do you think that the scene on the Day of Pentecost would have taken place? Don't you think that Peter would have stood up there and beat against the air, while the Jews would have gnashed their teeth and mocked him? But they tarried in Jerusalem; they waited ten days.

"What!" you say. "What, the world perishing and men dying! How can I wait?" But you must do what God tells you. There is no use in going before you are sent; there is no use in attempting to do God's work without God's power. A man working without this anointing, a man working without the Holy Spirit upon him, is losing his time, after all. On the other hand, he will not lose anything if he will tarry until he gets this power. That is the mark of true service: to wait on God, to tarry until we receive this power for witness-bearing.

On the Day of Pentecost, ten days after Jesus Christ was glorified, the Holy Spirit descended in power. Do you think that Peter and James and John and the other apostles doubted it from that very hour? No, they never doubted it. Yet, perhaps some people question the possibility of having the power of God now. They wonder whether the Holy Spirit ever came afterward in a similar manifestation and whether He will ever come again in such power.

But, if you turn to Acts 4:31, you will find that He came a second time, at a place where they were, so that the earth was shaken, and they were filled with His power. The fact is, we are leaky vessels, and we have to keep ourselves under the fountain all the time in order to keep ourselves full of Christ and so have a fresh supply of His power and His grace.

I believe this is a mistake a great many of us are making: We are trying to do God's work with the grace God gave us ten years ago. We say that, if it is necessary, we will go on with the same grace. Now, what we need is a fresh supply, a fresh anointing, and fresh power, and if we will seek it, and seek it with all our hearts, we will obtain it.

The early converts were taught to look for that power. Philip went to Samaria and news reached Jerusalem that there was a great work being done in Samaria and that there were many converts. As a result, John and Peter went to Samaria and laid their hands on the people there, and the people received the Holy Spirit for service. (See Acts 8:14–17.) I think that is what we Christians ought to be looking for—the Spirit of God for service—so that God may use us mightily in the building up of His church and hastening of His glory.

In Acts 19 we read of twelve men at Ephesus who, when the inquiry was made if they had received the Holy Spirit since they believed, answered, *"We have not so much as heard whether there be any Holy Ghost"* (v. 2). I venture to say there are very many people who, if you were to ask them, "Have you received the Holy Spirit since you believed?" would reply, "I don't know what you mean by that." They would be like the twelve men at Ephesus, who had never understood the particular relation of the Spirit to the sons of God in this dispensation.

I firmly believe that the church has laid this knowledge aside, misplaced it somewhere, and, as a result, Christians are without power. Sometimes you can bring one hundred members into the church, and they don't add to its power. Now, that is all wrong. If only the hundred new members were anointed by the Spirit of God, there would be great power in that church.

Green Fields

When I was out in California, the first time I went down from the Sierra Nevada Mountains and into the valley of the Sacramento River, I was surprised to find on one farm that everything about it was green—all the trees and flowers were blooming, and everything was green and beautiful. However, just across the hedge, everything was dried up. There was not a green thing there, and I could not understand it. I made inquiries, and I found that the man who had everything green had irrigated his land; he just poured the water right on, and he kept everything green. On the other hand, the fields that were next to his were as dry as Gideon's fleece, without a drop of dew. (See Judges 6:39–40.)

And so it is with many people in the church today. They are like these farms in California: dreary deserts, everything parched and desolate, with apparently no life in them. They can sit next to a man who is full of the Spirit of God, who is like a green bay tree, who is bringing forth fruit, yet they will not seek a similar blessing. Well, why this difference? Because God has poured water on the one who was thirsty; that is the difference. One has been seeking this anointing, and he has received it; the other has not been seeking, and so he has not received. When we want this anointing above everything else, God will surely give it to us.

The great question before us now is, Do we want it? I remember when I went to England and gave a Bible reading. I think it was the first reading that I gave in that country. A great many ministers were there. I didn't know anything about English theology, and I was afraid I would run against their creeds. As a result, I was a little hampered, especially on this very subject, about the gift of the Holy Spirit for service.

I particularly remember a Christian minister there who had his head bowed on his hand, and I thought the good man was ashamed of everything I was saying, and, of course, that troubled me. At the close of my address, he took his hat and went away, and then I thought, "Well, I shall never see him again." At the next meeting, I looked all around for him, and he wasn't there. At the next meeting, I looked again, but he was absent. I thought my teaching must have given him offense.

But a few days after that, at a large prayer meeting, a man stood up, and his face shone as if he had been up in the mountain with God. (See Exodus 34:29–30.) I looked at him, and to my great joy it was this brother. He said that he had been at that Bible reading and that he had heard there was such a thing as having fresh power to preach the Gospel. He said he made up his mind that if that was for him, he would have it. He said that he had gone home and looked to the Master, and that he had never in his life had such a battle with himself. He asked that God would show him the sinfulness of his heart that he knew nothing about, and he just cried mightily to God that he might be emptied of himself and filled with the Spirit. And then he said, "God has answered my prayer."

I met him in Edinburgh six months from that date, and he told me he had preached the Gospel every night during that time. In fact, after every sermon he had preached, some people had remained for conversation. He also had four months of upcoming engagements to preach the Gospel every night in different churches. I think that before this preacher got this anointing, you could have fired a cannon ball right through his church and not hit anyone; but, once he received the power, not even thirty days had passed before the building was full and the aisles crowded. He had his bucket filled full of fresh water, and the people found out about it and came flocking to him from every direction. I tell you, you can't get the stream higher than the fountain. What we need very specially is this power.

I also remember another man, who said, "I have heart disease; I can't preach more than once a week." He had a colleague preach for him and do the visiting. He was an old minister, so he couldn't do any visiting. He had heard of this anointing, and said, "I would like to be anointed for my burial. I would like, before I go hence, to have just one more privilege to preach the Gospel with power." He prayed that God would fill him with the Spirit. When I met him not long after that, he said, "I have preached on an average eight times a week, and I have had conversions, all along." The Spirit had come upon him.

I believe that this man broke down at first, not from too much hard work, but from using the machinery without oil, without lubrication. It is not the hard work that breaks down ministers, but it is the struggle of working without power. Oh, that God would anoint His people! Not only ministers, but also every disciple. Do not suppose that pastors are the only laborers needing it. There is not a mother who does not need it in her house to regulate her family, just as much as the minister needs it in the pulpit or the Sunday school teacher needs it in his Sunday school class. We all need it, together. Let us not rest, day or night, until we possess it. Let us say, "God helping me, I will not rest until endued with power from on high." (See Luke 24:49.) If that is the uppermost thought in our hearts, if we just hunger and thirst for it, God will give it to us.

Master and Servant

There is a very sweet story of Elijah and Elisha, and I love to dwell upon it. The time had come for Elijah to be taken up, and he said to Elisha, "You stay here at Gilgal, and I will go up to Bethel." (See 2 Kings 2:1–2.) There was a theological seminary there, and some young students, and he wanted to see how they were getting along. But Elisha said, *"As the Lord liveth, and as thy soul liveth, I will not leave thee"* (v. 2). And so Elisha remained close to Elijah. They came to Bethel, and the sons of the prophets came out and said to Elisha, "Do you know that your master is to be taken away?" And Elisha said, "I know it; but you keep still." (See verse 3.)

Then Elijah said to Elisha, "You remain at Bethel, while I go to Jericho." But Elisha said, *"As the Lord liveth, and as thy soul liveth, I will not leave thee"* (v. 4). Essentially, what Elisha said was, "You shall not go without me." I can imagine that Elisha just put his arm in that of Elijah, and they walked down together. I can see those two mighty men walking down to Jericho. When they arrived there, the sons of the prophets came and said to Elisha, "Do you know that your master is to be taken away?" "Hush! Keep still," said Elisha. "I know it." (See 2 Kings 2:5.)

And then Elijah said to Elisha, "Tarry here awhile; for the Lord has sent me to Jordan." But Elisha said, "As the Lord lives and my soul lives, I will not leave you. You shall not go without me." (See verse 6.) And then Elisha came right close to Elijah, and, as they went walking down, I imagine Elisha was after something. When they came to the Jordan, Elijah took off his mantle and struck the waters, and they separated hither and thither, and the two passed through like giants, dry-shod. (See verse 8.) Fifty sons of the prophets came to look at them and watch them. They didn't know that Elijah would be taken up right in their sight.

As they passed over the Jordan, Elijah said to Elisha, "Now, what do you want?" He knew that Elisha was after something. "What can I do for you? Just make your request known." And Elisha said, "I would like a double portion of the Spirit." (See verse 9.) I can imagine, now that Elijah had given him a chance to ask, he said to himself, "I will ask for enough." Elisha had a good deal of the Spirit, but he said, *I pray thee, let a double portion of thy spirit be upon me* (v. 9).

"Well," said Elijah, "if you see me when I am taken up, you shall have it." (See verse 10.) Do you think you could have enticed Elisha to walk apart from Elijah at that moment? I can almost see the two arm in arm, walking along, and as they walked, there came along the chariot of fire. Before Elisha knew it, Elijah was caught up, and as he went sweeping toward the throne, the servant cried, *"My father, my father, the chariot of Israel, and the horsemen thereof!"* (v. 12). Elisha saw him no more. He picked up Elijah's fallen mantle, and, returning with that old mantle of his master's, he came to the Jordan and cried for Elijah's God. The waters separated hither and thither, and he passed through, dry-shod. Then the watching prophets lifted up their voices and said, *"The Spirit of Elijah doth rest on Elisha"* (v. 15), and so a double portion of the Spirit was given.

May the Spirit of Elijah, beloved reader, be upon us. If we seek it, we will have it. Oh, may the God of Elijah answer by fire, consume the spirit of worldliness in the churches, burn up the dross, and make us wholehearted Christians. May that Spirit come upon us; let that be our prayer upon our family altars and in our prayer closets. Let us cry mightily to God that we may have a double portion of the Holy Spirit and that we may not rest satisfied with this worldly state of living. Let us, like Samson, shake ourselves and come out from the world, that we may have the power of God.

Chapter Five

Witnessing in Power

Chapter Five

Witnessing in Power

The subject of witness bearing in the power of the Holy Spirit is not sufficiently understood by the church. Until we have more understanding on this matter, we are laboring under great disadvantage. Now, if you will take your Bible and turn to John 15:26, you will find these words:

> *But when the Comforter is come, whom I will send unto you from the Father, even the Spirit of truth, which proceedeth from the Father, he shall testify of me: and ye also shall bear witness, because ye have been with me from the beginning.* (John 15:26–27)

Here we find what Christ said the Spirit would do when He came, namely, that He would testify of

Him. When Peter stood up on the Day of Pentecost and testified of what Christ had done, the Holy Spirit came down and bore witness to that fact, and men were convicted by hundreds and by thousands. (See Acts 2.) So then, man cannot preach effectively on his own. He must have the Spirit of God in order to receive ability, and he must study God's Word in order to testify according to the mind of the Spirit.

What Is the Testimony?

If we keep back the Gospel of Christ and do not bring Christ to the people, then the Spirit does not have the opportunity to work. But the moment Peter stood up on the Day of Pentecost and bore testimony to the fact that Christ died for sin and that He had risen again and ascended into heaven, the Spirit came down to bear witness to the person and work of Christ.

He came down to bear witness to the fact that Christ is in heaven; and if it were not for the Holy Spirit bearing witness to the preaching of the facts of the Gospel, do you think that the church would have lived during these last nineteen centuries? Do you believe that Christ's death, resurrection, and ascension would not have been forgotten as quickly as His birth was forgotten, if it had not been for the fact that the Holy Spirit had come?

It is very clear that when John made his appearance on the borders of the wilderness, people had forgotten all about the birth of Jesus Christ. Just thirty short years had passed, and it was all gone. They had forgotten the story of the shepherds; they had forgotten the wonderful scene that took place in the temple, when the Son of God was brought into the temple and the older prophets and prophetesses were there; they had forgotten about the wise men coming to Jerusalem to inquire where they could find He who was born King of the Jews. That story of His birth seemed to have just faded away; they had forgotten all about it, and when John made his appearance on the borders of the wilderness, it was brought back to their minds. If it had not been for the Holy Spirit coming down to bear witness to Christ, to testify of His death and resurrection, these facts would have been forgotten as soon as His birth.

Greater Work

The witness of the Spirit is the witness of power. Jesus said:

He that believeth on me, the works that I do shall he do also; and greater works than these shall he do; because I go unto my Father.

(John 14:12)

I used to stumble over that. I didn't understand it. I thought, "What greater work could any man do than Christ had done? How could anyone raise a dead man who had been laid away in the sepulchre for days, and who had already begun to turn back to dust; how with a word could he call him forth?" But the longer I live, the more I am convinced it is an even greater thing to influence a man's will, a man whose will is set against God. It is greater to have that will broken and brought into subjection to God's will—or, in other words, it is a greater thing to have power over a living, sinning, God-hating man—than to quicken the dead.

He who could create a world could speak a dead soul into life, but I think the greatest miracle this world has ever seen was the miracle at Pentecost. Here were men who surrounded the apostles, men who were full of prejudice, full of malice, full of bitterness—their hands, as it were, dripping with the blood of the Son of God. And yet, an unlettered man, a man whom they detested, a man whom they hated, stood up there and preached the Gospel, and three thousand of them were immediately convicted and converted, became disciples of the Lord Jesus Christ, and were willing to lay down their lives for the Son of God.

It may have been on that occasion that Stephen, the first martyr, was converted, as well as some of the men who soon after gave up their lives for Christ. This seems to me the greatest miracle the world has ever seen. But Peter did not labor alone; the Spirit of God was with him—hence the marvelous results.

The Jewish law required that there should be at least two witnesses (see Deuteronomy 17:6 and

19:15), and so we find that when Peter preached, there was a second witness. Peter testified of Christ, and Christ said, "When the Holy Spirit comes, He will testify of Me." (See John 15:26.) Thus, both Peter and the Holy Spirit bore witness to the verities of our Lord's incarnation, ministry, death, and resurrection, and the result was that a multitude turned as with one heart unto the Lord.

Our failure now is that preachers ignore the Cross, and they veil Christ with sapless sermons and superfine language. They don't just present Him to the people plainly, and that is why I believe that the Spirit of God doesn't work with power in our churches. What we need is to preach Christ and to present Him to a perishing world. The world can get on very well without you and me, but the world cannot get on without Christ, and, therefore, we must testify of Him.

I believe that the world today is just hungering and thirsting for this divine, satisfying portion. Thousands and thousands are sitting in darkness, knowing nothing of this great Light. But when we begin to preach Christ honestly, faithfully, sincerely, and truthfully—holding Him up and not ourselves, exalting Christ and not our theories, presenting Christ and not our opinions, advocating Christ and not some fake doctrine—then the Holy Spirit will come and bear witness. He will testify that what we say is true.

When He comes, He will confirm the Lord with signs that will follow. (See Mark 16:20.) This is one of the strongest proofs that our Gospel is divine and that it is of divine origin. Not only did Christ teach these things, but, when leaving the world, He said, *"He shall glorify me"* (John 16:14), and, *"He shall testify of me"* (John 15:26).

If you will look at the second chapter of Acts, to that wonderful sermon Peter preached, you will read these words:

> *Therefore let all the house of Israel know assuredly, that God hath made that same Jesus, whom ye have crucified, both Lord and Christ.*
> (Acts 2:36)

And when Peter said this, the Holy Spirit descended upon the people and testified of Christ. The Spirit bore witness in signal demonstration that all this was true. And again, in the fortieth verse, *"And with many other words did he testify and exhort, saying, Save yourselves from this untoward generation."* The Holy Spirit testified with many other words—not only with these words that have been recorded, but also with many other words.

The Sure Guide

> *Howbeit when he, the Spirit of truth, is come, he will guide you into all truth: for he shall not speak of himself; but whatsoever he shall hear, that shall he speak: and he will show you things to come.* (John 16:13)

"He will guide you into all truth." Now, there is no truth that we need to know that the Spirit of God will not guide us into if we will let Him. If we will yield ourselves up to be directed by the Spirit and let Him lead us, He will guide us into all truth. It would have saved us from a great many dark hours if we had only been willing to let the Spirit of God be our Counselor and Guide.

Lot never would have gone to Sodom if he had been guided by the Spirit of God. David never would have fallen into sin and had all that trouble with his family if he had been guided by the Spirit of God. There are many Lots and Davids even today. The churches are full of them. Men and women are in total darkness because they have not been willing to be guided by the Spirit of God. *"He will guide you into all truth: for he shall not speak of himself"* (John 16:13). He shall speak of the ascended, glorified Christ.

What would be thought of a messenger, who, entrusted by an absent husband with a message for his wife, talked only of himself and his ideas upon arrival, ignoring both the husband and the message? You would simply call it outrageous. What, then, must be the crime of the professed teacher who speaks of himself, or some insipid theory, leaving out Christ and His Gospel? If we witness according to the Spirit, we must also bear witness of Jesus.

The Holy Spirit is down here in this dark world to speak of the One who is absent, and He takes the things of Christ and brings them to our minds. (See John 14:26.) He testifies of Christ; He guides us into the truth about Him.

Rappings in the Dark

I will take a moment here to express my opinion on something. I think that, in this day, a great many children of God are turning aside and committing a grievous sin. I don't know if they think it is a sin, but if we examine the Scriptures, I am sure we will find that it is a great sin. What is this sin that I am hinting at?

We are told that the Comforter is sent into the world to guide us into all truth. (See John 16:13.) If He is sent for that purpose, do we need any other guide? Do we need to hide in the darkness, consulting with mediums, who profess to call up the spirits of the dead? Many people, however, are deceived by such false guides. Do you know what the Word of God pronounces against that fearful sin? I believe it is one of the greatest sins we have to contend with in the present day. It would be dishonoring to the Holy Spirit for me to go and summon up the dead and confer with them, even if it were possible.

I would like you to notice a passage in 1 Chronicles 10:

> So Saul died for his transgression which he had committed against the LORD, even against the word of the LORD, which he kept not, and also

for asking counsel of one that had a familiar spirit, to inquire of it; and inquired not of the LORD: therefore he slew him, and turned the kingdom unto David the son of Jesse.

(vv. 13–14)

God slew Saul for this very sin of which I write. Of the two sins that are brought against Saul here, one is that he would not listen to the Word of God, and the second is that he consulted a familiar spirit, or a spirit of the dead. He was snared by this great evil, and so he sinned against God.

Saul fell short at this point, and there are a great many of God's professed children today who think there is no harm in consulting a medium who pretends to call up some of the departed to inquire of them. But how dishonoring it is to God, who has sent the Holy Spirit into this world to guide us into all truth! There is not a thing that I need to know, there is not a thing that is important for me to know, there is not a thing that I ought to know, that the Spirit of God will not reveal to me through the Word of God.

If I turn my back on the Holy Spirit, I am dishonoring the Spirit of God, and I am committing a grievous sin. In the gospel of Luke, there is a story of a rich man in the other world who wanted to have someone sent to his father's house to warn his five brothers. Christ said, *"They have Moses and the prophets....If they hear not* [them], *neither will they be persuaded, though one rose from the dead"* (Luke 16:29,

31). Moses and the prophets, or the part of the Bible then completed, should have been enough, and even today the Scriptures should be enough. But a great many people now want something besides the Word of God, and so they are turning aside to these false lights.

Spirits That Peep and Mutter

There is another passage in Scripture that reads,

> *And when they shall say unto you, Seek unto them that have familiar spirits, and unto wizards that peep, and that mutter: should not a people seek unto their God? for the living to the dead?* (Isa. 8:19)

What is that but table-rapping and cabinet-hiding? If what you needed to hear was a message from God, do you think you would have to go into a dark room and turn out all the lights? My Master taught nothing in secret. (See John 18:20.) God is not in that movement, and what we need, as children of God, is to keep ourselves from this evil.

Notice, also, the following verse in Isaiah, quoted so often out of its context:

> *To the law and to the testimony: if they speak not according to this word, it is because there is no light in them.* (Isa. 8:20)

Let us understand that anyone who comes to us with any doctrine that is not according to the law and the testimony is from the Evil One and is an enemy of righteousness. He has no light in him.

Now, you will discover that these people who are consulting familiar spirits, first and last, attack the Word of God. They don't believe it. A great many people say that you must hear both sides. But, if a man should write me a slanderous letter about my wife, I don't think I would have to read it; I would tear it up and throw it to the winds. Do I have to read all the infidel books that are written in order to hear both sides? Do I have to take up a book that is a slander against my Lord and Master, who has redeemed me with His blood? Ten thousand times, no; I will not touch it.

Here is my point in clear language:

Now the Spirit speaketh expressly, that in the latter times some shall depart from the faith, giving heed to seducing spirits, and doctrines of devils; speaking lies in hypocrisy; having their conscience seared with a hot iron.

(1 Tim. 4:1–2)

Doctrines of devils. Could this be any clearer? There are other passages of Scripture that warn against every delusion of Satan, but this is sufficient for now.

Let us always remember that the Spirit has been sent into the world to guide us into all truth.

(See John 16:13.) We don't need any other guide; He is enough. Some people say, "Is not conscience a safer guide than the Word and the Spirit?" No, it is not. Some people don't seem to have any conscience, and they don't know what it means. Their education has a good deal to do with conscience. There are people who will say that their conscience did not tell them that they had done wrong until after the wrong was done. But what we need is something to tell us that a thing is wrong before we do it. Very often, a man will go and commit some awful crime. After it is done, his conscience will wake up and lash and scourge him. But then it is too late; the act is done.

The Unerring Guide

I am told by people who have been over the Alps that, if they are going in a dangerous place, the guide fastens them right to himself, and he just goes on before them; they are fastened to the guide.

And so should the Christian be linked to God's unerring Guide and be safely upheld. If a man was going through the Mammoth Cave, it would be death to him if he strayed away from his guide; if separated from him, he would certainly perish. There are pitfalls in that cave and a bottomless river, and there would be no chance for a man to find his way through that cave without a guide or a light.

Likewise, there is no chance for us to get through the dark wilderness of this world alone. It is folly for a man or woman to think that he or she can get through this evil world without the light of God's Word and the guidance of the divine Spirit. God sent Him to guide us through this great journey, and if we seek to walk independently of Him, we will stumble into the deep darkness of eternity's night.

But you must always bear in mind the words of the Spirit of God if you want to be guided. You must study the Word, because the Word is the light of the Spirit. In John 14:26 we read,

> *But the Comforter, which is the Holy Ghost, whom the Father will send in my name, he shall teach you all things, and bring all things to your remembrance, whatsoever I have said unto you.*

And John 16:13 says,

> *Howbeit when he, the Spirit of truth, is come, he will guide you into all truth: for he shall not speak of himself; but whatsoever he shall hear, that shall he speak: and he will show you things to come.*

"He will show you things to come." A great many people seem to think that the Bible is out-of-date, that it is an old book; they think it has passed its day. They say it was very good for the Dark Ages

and that there is some very good history in it. But they also say it was not intended for the present time, that we are living in a very enlightened age, and that men can get on very well without the old Book; we have outgrown it. They think we have no use for it because it is an old book. Now, you might just as well say that the sun, which has shone so long, is now so old that it is out-of-date, and that, whenever a man builds a house, he need not put any windows in it, because we have a newer and better light. We have gas lighting and electricity, and these are relatively new.

Yet, if people don't see the absurdity of this, if they still think the Bible is too old and worn out, I would advise them not to put any windows in their houses when they build them. Instead, they should just light them with electric light; that is something new enough, and the new is what they are anxious to have.

But what ridiculous advice! People talk about the Bible as if they understand it, but we don't know much about it yet. Every day we can read in our newspapers about what has taken place. This Bible, however, tells us what is about to take place. This *is* new; we have the news right here in this Book.

The Bible tells us of the things that will surely come to pass, and that is a great deal newer than anything in the newspapers. It tells us that the Spirit will teach us all things; not only will He guide us into all truth, but He will also teach us all things. He teaches us how to pray, and I don't think there has ever been a prayer upon this sin-cursed earth, inspired by the Holy Spirit, that was not answered. But there is also much praying that is not inspired by the Holy Spirit.

In years gone by, I was very ambitious to get rich. I used to pray for one hundred thousand dollars; that was my goal. I used to say, "God does not answer my prayer; He is not making me rich." But I had no warrant for such a prayer. That is the case with many people: They pray in that way; they think that they are praying, but they do not pray according to the Scriptures. The Spirit of God has nothing to do with their prayers, and such prayers are not the product of His teaching.

It is also the Spirit who teaches us how to answer our enemies. If a man strikes me, I should not pull out a gun and shoot him. The Spirit of the Lord doesn't teach me revenge; He doesn't teach me that it is necessary to draw the sword and cut a man down in order to defend my rights. Some people say, "You are a coward if you don't strike back." Christ says, "Turn the other cheek to him who smites." (See Matthew 5:39.) I would rather take Christ's teaching than any other. I don't think a man gains much by loading himself down with weapons to defend himself. Enough lives have been sacrificed in this country to teach men a lesson in this.

The Word of God is a much better protection than the gun. We would do well to take the Word of

God to protect us, by accepting its teaching and by living out its precepts. We would do well to let the Holy Spirit be our guide.

An Aid to Memory

It is a great comfort to us to remember that another office of the Spirit is to bring the teaching of Jesus to our remembrance. This was our Lord's promise: *"He shall teach you all things, and bring all things to your remembrance"* (John 14:26). This is a very powerful statement.

I think there are many Christians who have had that experience. When they have been testifying of Christ and while they have been witnessing for Him, they have found that the Spirit has just brought to their minds some of the sayings of the Lord Jesus Christ, and their minds were soon filled with the Word of God. When we have the Spirit of God resting upon us, we can speak with authority and power, and the Lord will bless our testimony and our work.

I believe the reason God makes use of so few in the church is that Christians do not have any power in them that God can use. We must have the Word of God, not our own ideas, hidden in our hearts. (See Psalm 119:11.) And then, with the Holy Spirit inflaming us, we will have a testimony that will be rich and sweet and fresh, and the Lord's Word will vindicate itself in blessed results.

God wants to use us; God wants to make us into channels of blessing, but we are in such a condition that He cannot use us. That is the trouble. There are so many men who have no testimony for the Lord; if they speak, they speak without saying anything, and if they pray, their prayers are powerless. They do not plead in prayer; their prayers are just a few set phrases that you have heard too often. Now, what we need is to be so full of the Word that the Spirit coming upon us will bring to our minds—bring to our remembrance—the words of the Lord Jesus.

In 1 Corinthians 2:9, it is written:

Eye hath not seen, nor ear heard, neither have entered into the heart of man, the things which God hath prepared for them that love him.

We hear that quoted so often in prayer; many a man weaves it into his prayer and stops right there. And the moment you talk about heaven, he will say, "Oh, I don't know anything about heaven; it has not entered into the heart of man. You know, *'eye hath not seen'*; it is all speculation; we have nothing to do with it."

And so, they say that they quote it as it is written: *"Eye hath not seen, nor ear heard, neither have entered into the heart of man, the things which God hath prepared for them that love him."* Yet, what is next? *"But God hath revealed them unto us by his Spirit"* (v. 10). You see, the Lord *has* revealed them to us: *"For the Spirit searcheth all things, yea, the deep things of God"* (v. 10). That is just what the Spirit does. He brings to our minds what God has in store for us.

Farsightedness and Nearsightedness

I heard a man, some time ago, speaking about Abraham. He said, "Abraham was not tempted by the well-watered plains of Sodom, for Abraham was what you might call a farsighted man; he had his eyes set on the city that has a foundation—*'whose builder and maker is God'* (Heb. 11:10)."

In contrast to Abraham, however, Lot was a nearsighted man. There are many people in the church who are very nearsighted; they only see the things right around them that they think are good. Abraham was farsighted; he had glimpses of the Celestial City. Moses was farsighted; he left the palaces of Egypt and identified himself with God's people—poor people, who were slaves—but he had something in view. He could see something that God had in store.

There are also some people who are sort of farsighted and nearsighted at the same time. I have a friend who has one farsighted eye and one nearsighted eye. I think the church is full of this kind of people. They use one eye for the world and the other for the kingdom of God. Therefore, everything is blurred and confusing. One eye is looking far and the other is looking near, and they *"see men as trees, walking"* (Mark 8:24). The church is filled with that sort of people.

But Stephen was farsighted; he looked clear into heaven. Even when he was dying, they couldn't convince him that Christ had not ascended to heaven. *"Behold,"* he said, *"I see the heavens opened, and the Son of man standing on the right hand of God"* (Acts 7:56), and he looked clear into heaven. The world had no temptation for him; he had put the world under his feet.

Paul was another of those farsighted men. He had been caught up to heaven and had seen things unlawful for him to utter—things grand and glorious. (See 2 Corinthians 12:2–4.) I tell you, when the Spirit of God is on us, the world looks very empty; the world has a very small hold upon us, and we begin to let go of it. When the Spirit of God is on us, we will just let go of the things of time and lay hold of things eternal. This is the need of the church today: We need the Spirit to come in mighty power, to consume all the vile dross there is in us. Oh, that the Spirit of fire would come down and burn everything in us that is contrary to God's blessed Word and will!

In John 14:16 we read of the Comforter. This is the first time He is spoken of as the Comforter. Christ had been the disciples' comforter until that time, but God sent the Spirit to comfort the sorrowing. It was prophesied:

The Spirit of the Lord is upon me, because he hath anointed me to preach the gospel to the poor; he hath sent me to heal the brokenhearted.

(Luke 4:18)

You can't heal the brokenhearted without the Comforter; but the world did not want the first Comforter, and so they rose up and took Him to Calvary and put Him to death. But on going away He said, "I will send you another Comforter; you shall not be comfortless; be of good cheer, little flock; it is the Father's good pleasure to give you the kingdom." (See John 14:16–18.) All these sweet passages are brought to the remembrance of God's people, and they help us to rise out of the fog and mist of this world. Oh, what a Comforter is the Holy Spirit of God!

The Faithful Friend

The Holy Spirit tells a man of his faults in order to lead him to a better life. In John 16:8 we read, *"He will reprove the world of sin."* Now, there is a class of people who don't like this part of the Spirit's work. Do you know why? Because He convicts them of sin; they don't like that. What they want is someone to speak comforting words and make everything pleasant; keep everything all quiet; tell them there is peace when there is war; tell them it is light when it is dark; tell them that the world is getting on amazingly in goodness, that it is getting better all the time. That is the kind of preaching they seek.

In these times, men think they are a great deal better than their fathers were. That suits human nature, for it is full of pride. Men will strut around and say, "Yes, I believe that. The world is improving, and I am a good deal better man than my father was. My father was too strict; he was one of those old puritanical men who were so rigid. Oh, we are getting on well; we are more liberal. My father wouldn't think of going out riding on Sunday, but we will; we will trample the laws of God under our feet; we are better than our fathers."

That is the kind of preaching that some people love, and there are preachers who tickle such itching ears. When you bring the Word of God to bear upon them, and when the Spirit drives it home, then men will say, "I don't like that kind of preaching; I will never go to hear that man again." And sometimes they will get up and stamp their way out of church before the speaker finishes; they don't like it. But when the Spirit of God is at work, He convicts men of sin. *When he is come, he will reprove the world of sin, and of righteousness, and of judgment: of sin*—not because men swear, lie, steal, and get drunk and murder, but—*"because they believe not on me"* (John 16:8–9).

The Determinative Sin

That is the sin of the world. A great many people think that unbelief is a sort of misfortune, but they do not know, if you will allow me the expression, that it is the damning sin of the world today. That is what unbelief is—the mother of all sin. There would not be a drunkard walking the streets if it were not for unbelief; there would not be a harlot walking the streets if it were not for unbelief; there would not be a murderer if it were not for unbelief. Unbelief is the beginning of all sin.

Don't think for a moment that unbelief is a misfortune. Rather, keep in mind that it is an awful sin, and may the Holy Spirit convict every reader that unbelief is the same as making God a liar. (See 1 John 1:10.) Many a man has been knocked down on the streets because someone has told him he was a liar. Unbelief is giving God the lie; that is the plain English of it.

Some people seem to boast of their unbelief; they seem to think it is quite respectable to be an infidel and to doubt God's Word, and they will vainly boast and say, "I have intellectual difficulties; I can't believe." Oh, that the Spirit of God would come and convict men of sin! That is what we need—His convicting power—and I am so thankful that God has not put that into our hands. We do not have the right or the responsibility to convict men; if we did, I would get discouraged and give up preaching and go back to the business world within the next forty-eight hours. It is my work to preach and hold up the Cross and to testify of Christ, but it is the work of the Spirit to convict men of sin and lead them to Christ.

One thing I have noticed is that some conversions don't amount to anything, that if a man professes to be converted without conviction of sin, he is one of those stony-ground hearers who don't bring forth much fruit. (See Matthew 13:3–6.) The first little wave of persecution, the first breath of opposition, and the man is back in the world again. Let us pray, dear Christian reader, that God may carry on a deep and thorough work, that men may be convicted of sin so that they cannot rest in unbelief. Let us pray to God that it may be a thorough work in the land.

I would rather see a hundred men thoroughly converted, truly born of God, than see a thousand professed conversions where the Spirit of God has not convicted of sin. Don't let us cry, "Peace, peace," when there is no peace. (See Jeremiah 6:14.) Don't let us go to the man who is living in sin and tell him all he has to do is stand right up and profess faith, without expressing any hatred for sin. Let us ask God first to show every man the plague of his own heart, so that the Spirit may convict all men of sin. Then the work in our hands will be real and deep and will abide the fiery trial that will try every man's labor.

> Holy Spirit, faithful guide,
>   Ever near the Christian's side;
> Gently lead us by the hand,
>   Pilgrims in a desert land;
>
> Weary souls for e'er rejoice,
>   While they hear that sweetest voice,

Whisp'ring softly, wanderer come!
    Follow Me, I'll guide thee home.

Ever present, truest Friend,
    Ever near thine aid to lend,
Leave us not to doubt and fear,
    Groping on in darkness drear,

When the storms are raging sore,
    Hearts grow faint, and hopes give o'er;
Whisp'ring softly, wanderer come!
    Follow Me, I'll guide thee home.

When our days of toil shall cease,
    Waiting still for sweet release,
Nothing left but heaven and prayer,
    Wond'ring if our names were there,

Wading deep the dismal flood,
    Pleading nought but Jesus' blood;
Whisp'ring softly, wanderer come!
    Follow Me, I'll guide thee home.

About the Author

D. L. Moody

About the Author

On February 5, 1837, in Northfield, Massachusetts, Dwight Lyman Moody was born, the sixth in what would be a family of nine children. His father died when Moody was only a tender child, leaving little provision for the family. Hence, Moody learned the value of hard work at an early age. An ambitious youth, Moody went to Boston at the age of seventeen, where he became a successful salesman in his uncle's shoe store. His uncle made him promise to go to church, a promise that he faithfully kept; as a result he was won to the Lord by his Sunday school teacher.

In 1856, Moody went to Chicago, where he continued to succeed as a shoe salesman. His fervor in selling shoes was exceeded, however, by his zeal in winning souls, and he began to pack the pews of the church with young men. At the age of twenty-three, he devoted himself to full-time Christian work. Because of his poor grammar, his first attempts at public speaking were not well received by all; one deacon told him that he would serve God best by keeping still. Nonetheless, Moody persevered, and he became famous nationwide for his Sunday school work. He was also known for his ministry to soldiers during the Civil War; many were brought to Christ through his meetings and his distribution of Bibles and tracts.

In 1867, Moody traveled to Great Britain to learn new methods in Christian work. It was there that his heart was stirred and forever changed by these words, spoken to him by a well-known evangelist: "The world has yet to see what God will do with...the man who is fully consecrated to Him." Moody determined to be that man.

The road of full commitment was not without trials. In 1871, the church that Moody pastored, the largest church in Chicago, was destroyed in the Chicago fire. But in the wake of this disaster, Moody received the filling of the Holy Spirit. Never before had he experienced such a mighty revelation of God's love. After this empowering of the Spirit, Moody went on to accomplish even more for Christ. He held meetings in America, England, and Scotland, where thousands attended and many were brought to Christ. He also founded Moody Bible Institute.

When Moody died in 1899, he left a rich legacy: three Christian schools, a Christian publishing business, and a million souls won for Christ. The day of his death was not a sad day; rather, Moody exclaimed, "This is my triumph; this is my coronation day!"

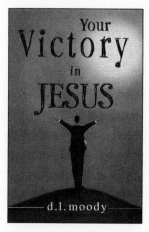

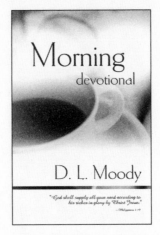